TEACH YOURSELF BOOKS

BRAZILIAN PORTUGUESE

A COMPLETE COURSE FOR BEGINNERS

BRAZILIAN PORTUGUESE

A COMPLETE COURSE FOR BEGINNERS

Sue Tyson-Ward

TEACH YOURSELF BOOKS

Dedication

For Mum and Dad

Acknowledgements

Many thanks to Mrs Lúcia Cooper for materials and guidance and, as ever, to Sarah Mitchell at Hodder for her total encouragement. And to Brazil, for instilling the fire of life. Viva!

Long-renowned as the authoritative source for self-guided learning – with more than 30 million copies sold worldwide – the *Teach Yourself* series includes over 200 titles in the fields of languages, crafts, hobbies, sports, and other leisure activities.

A catalogue record for this title is available from the British Library.

Library of Congress Catalog Card Number: 96-72377

First published in UK 1997 by Hodder Headline Plc, 338 Euston Road, London NW1 3BH

First published in US 1997 by NTC Publishing Group
An imprint of NTC/Contemporary Publishing Company
4255 West Touhy Avenue, Lincolnwood (Chicago), Illinois 60646-1975 U.S.A.

Typeset by Transet Limited, Coventry, England.
Printed in England by Cox & Wyman Limited, Reading, Berkshire.

Impression number 10 9 8 7 6 5 4 3 2 1
Year 2000 1999 1998 1997 1997

CONTENTS

— INTRODUCTION —

This course is designed for the absolute beginner and requires no previous knowledge of any foreign language. The aim of the course is to enable you to use Brazilian Portuguese in everyday situations and also to provide some background information about Brazil and Brazilian culture.

The Portuguese of Brazil is different from that of Continental Portugal in three main ways: vocabulary, grammatical structures, and, most important, pronunciation. You could consider the two variants of the language in the same way as American and British English. It is widely considered that Brazilian Portuguese is actually easier to understand than European, as the Portuguese speak very quickly, with their mouths closed very much around the words, and they often 'eat' the beginning and ending of words. If you are learning Brazilian Portuguese, be assured that people will understand what you are saying (apart from the odd few words) throughout the Portuguese-speaking world. It is important for you to understand that you are not learning 'Brazilian', but 'Brazilian Portuguese'. It is surprising how many people (including some native speakers) believe 'Brazilian' is actually a language. It is not, it is a *variant* of the Portuguese language.

Portuguese is not a difficult language to take on board if you have had some experience of another Latin-based (or Romance) language, such as French, Spanish or Italian. Pronunciation is the main area you will need to concentrate on. Many people erroneously believe that, as it looks like Spanish, it will sound that way too. Constant practice with the cassette will help you improve in this respect. If you have no knowledge of a Romance language, or in fact, of *any* language, take heart – you are starting out with a clean slate and with no preconceptions which could mislead you.

The American influence on Brazil, via TV and other mass-media communications has resulted in various English words entering the Brazilian speaker's vocabulary; words such as *shopping*, *flat* and *short* (*shorts*) are commonplace today.

How to use this book

Each of the 18 units is structured as follows:

Introduction. An introduction in English that explains what you will learn in the unit.

Diálogo. There are dialogues at the beginning of each chapter, and sometimes later on. Using the cassette, listen to them first to check the pronunciation and see how much you understand, then read them carefully, and if necessary, listen again.

Vocabulário. The vocabulary section that follows each dialogue contains the new words and expressions that you will need to understand it.

Verdadeiro ou falso? *(True or false?)*. These are statements about the texts in either English or Portuguese that may be *true* or *false*. The aim of these exercises is to check whether you have understood the text.

Dicas Culturais. Hints or tips – comments on life and society as well as background information on Brazil.

Sumário. The important words and expressions used in the dialogues are repeated here.

Gramática. Notes explaining grammatical structures and how to create your own sentences.

Exercícios/Atividades. In these you practise the new words and information you have learnt.

Compreende? *(Do you understand?)* Further dialogues and texts, testing your comprehension. These are not designed to test every word, but to give you the opportunity to 'get the gist' of a text.

In addition, the symbol indicates material included on the accompanying cassette.

The best way to make progress is to work a little every day. Listen to the cassette and read the dialogues several times, learning the vocabulary before you start the exercises. Try to devise interesting ways to memorise the new words, such as through picture-images, songs, rhymes, etc.

Teach Yourself Brazilian Portuguese follows the journey of Sylvia Peters on a 6-month trip to Brazil, as she endeavours to make social, cultural and business links for future exchange. During the course of her journey you, like her, will visit some of Brazil's most important cities, and be introduced to its people, history and culture. Initially, Sylvia will be the guest of the Ferreira family; José is a marine biologist, and Marlí teaches Portuguese in a language school. Sylvia returns to their house before leaving Brazil for the UK.

— PRONUNCIATION —

Although this book can successfully be used on its own, the purchase of the cassette will enhance both your pronunciation and your comprehension abilities as well as giving you the opportunity for aural revision.

In native Portuguese words there is no **k**, **w**, or **y**, although they appear in imported words. Pronunciation in Brazil varies from region to region, as it may do in any country. There are certain distinct sounds in Rio which mark the speaker as a 'Carioca' (a native of Rio), e.g. the **de** sound at the end of a word pronounced as **gee**.

The whole Portuguese alphabet is as follows. If you have the cassette, listen to how it sounds when recited in Portuguese.

a b c d e f g h i j (k) l m n o p q r s t
u v (w) x (y) z

Portuguese vowels

Portuguese vowel sounds are tricky to imitate, as there are nasal sounds, and sounds differ depending on where the vowel is in any given word. However, Brazilians do open their mouths wider than the Portuguese, and are therefore theoretically easier to understand! Here is a general idea:

a, as in *rather* – **falar**	or as in *abide* – **mesa**
ã, as in *rang* – **irmã**.	This is a nasal sound.
e, as in *bell* – **certo**	or as in *madden* – **pesar**

i, as in *mean* – **partida**	or as in *cigar* – **emigrar**
o, as in *saw* – **nova**	or as in *boot* – **sapato**
u, as in *boot* – **durmo**	or as in *bull* – **mudar**

Portuguese consonants

Portuguese consonants also differ from the English sounds in different situations. Follow the table on the cassette, if you have it, as each consonant is given an English equivalent, and a Portuguese example:

Consonant	**English sound**	**Portuguese sound**
b	*ball*	bonito
c+e/i, ç	*sat*	cem, começa
c+a/o/u	*can*	comer
ch	*shout*	chocolate
d	*dab*	dar or cidade
f	*fun*	falar
g + e/i	*pleasure*	geléia
g + a/o/u	*got*	pagar
h	'silent'	hotel
j	*pleasure*	julho
l	*last*	livre/total
lh	*billion*	mulher
m	*map*	mesa
n	*nod*	nadar
nh	*onion*	vinho
p	*pin*	parar
q (u)	*quart*	quando
q(u) + e/i	'silent u'	quem
r (initial)	'aspirated'	rio
r	*ran*	compram
s	*sat*	sol
s + vowels	*zoo*	casa
t	*tap*	todo
v	'as in English'	vida
x	*shout*	baixa
z	*zoo/shout*	fazer/faz

The stress rules

Portuguese words are stressed on the last syllable if they end in **i**, **u**, diphthongs, consonants, and nasal vowels, e.g. **papel**, **irmão**.

They are stressed on the syllable before last if they are verbs ending in **am** or **em**, or words ending in **a**, **e**, **o**, **em**, **ens** – **mesa**, **falam**.

If a word breaks either of these rules, a written accent is added to show where the stress falls. So if you see a word with a written accent, you must stress the syllable where the accent is placed.

A few tips to help you acquire an authentic accent

It is not absolutely vital to acquire a perfect accent. The aim is to be understood; here are a number of techniques for working on your pronunciation:

1. Listen carefully to the cassette or native speaker or teacher. Whenever possible repeat aloud imagining you are a native speaker of Portuguese.
2. Tape record yourself and compare your pronunciation with that of a native speaker.
3. Ask native speakers to listen to your pronunciation and tell you how to improve it.
4. Ask native speakers how a specific sound is formed. Watch them and practise at home in front of a mirror.
5. Make a list of words that give you pronunciation trouble and practise them.

1

SEU PASSAPORTE POR FAVOR

Your passport please

In this unit you will learn

- how to identify people
- how to introduce yourself and address people
- how to say hello and goodbye
- how to check into your hotel

Diálogo 1 *Dialogue 1*

Sylvia Peters arrives in Brazil and passes through Customs (**Alfândega**).

Inspetor Bom dia. Seu passaporte por favor.
Sylvia Aqui está.
Inspetor Você é inglesa, não é?
Sylvia Sim, sou.
Inspetor Muito bem. Quanto tempo vai passar aqui?
Sylvia Seis meses.
Inspetor Está bem. Obrigado. Tchau.
Sylvia Bom dia, obrigada.

bom dia *hello, good morning* (also *goodbye*)
seu *your*
passaporte (o) *passport*
por favor *please*
aqui, cá *here*
está *(it) is*
você *you*
é *is/are*
inglesa *English* (woman)

não é? *isn't it/is that so?*
não *no,not*
sim *yes*
sou *I am*
muito bem *very well*
vai passar *you're going to spend*
quanto? *how much?*
tempo(o) *time*
seis *six*
meses(os) *months*
está bem *OK*
obrigado/a *thank you*
tchau *see you/bye*

Verdadeiro ou falso? *True or false?*

Tick true (*verdadeiro*) or false (*falso*) for the following statements based on the dialogue.

	V	F
(*a*) Sylvia Peters is American.		
(*b*) She's going to spend six weeks in Brazil.		
(*c*) She arrives in the morning.		

Gramática *Grammar*

1 *To be*

In Portuguese there are two verbs both meaning **To Be**:

Ser is used for permanent characteristics, such as nationality. **Estar** is used more for temporary states and locations.

In the dialogue you saw examples of both verbs:

aqui está	*here it is*	**ESTAR**
você é inglesa	*you are English*	**SER**
sim, sou	*yes I am*	**SER**
está bem	*that's OK*	**ESTAR**

You will come across more examples, and find out other ways in which the verbs are used, as you work through the Units.

2 *Forms of address:* Você

In Brazil, most people call each other *you* using the word **você**. However, there are certain situations where more, or less, formality in address is called for. Look at the table below to see how these differences work.

SITUATION	FORMAL YOU	INFORMAL YOU
With strangers, people in higher social/work position	**o senhor** (to man) **a senhora** (to woman)	
With friends, colleagues, family		**você/tu** (some parts of Brazil)
With older people	**o senhor/a senhora**	

Você and **tu** are examples of what are called Personal Pronouns – the words for *I*, *you*, *he*, etc.

3 Personal Pronouns

The Portuguese Personal Pronouns are used to denote which person is carrying out the action of a verb. They are:

EU	*I*	**NÓS**	*We*
(TU)	*You* [used only in some parts of Brazil]		
ELE	*He / it*	**ELES**	*They (male)*
ELA	*She / it*	**ELAS**	*They (female)*
VOCÊ	*You*	**VOCÊS**	*You (plural)*

These are referred to as Subject Pronouns, but they are not necessarily used all the time; in many instances the endings of the verbs will suffice to tell you who is doing the action. In the dialogue you had:

é inglesa *you are English*
sim, sou *yes, I am*

You will learn more of verbs later on.

4 Male/Female

In Portuguese, everything you see around you is divided into two groups: masculine and feminine. This is because Portuguese is a language with its roots in Latin, and the Romans used a language system based on words linking together, usually in a logical way (although it may not seem so to many learners!). So, for example, a table happens to be a feminine word, and the floor is a masculine one. In most cases you can tell which group a word belongs to by its ending: an **-o** for masculine words, and an **-a** for feminine ones, although this is not always the case. A dictionary will guide you when you are first learning, and look for help in the vocabulary lists, until you start to get a feel for the different endings.

5 Obrigado/a

You will have noticed in the dialogue that the Customs official says **Obrigado**, and Sylvia replies **Obrigada**, both meaning *Thank you*. All men should use the first and women the second, regardless of whom they are addressing. This is because Obrigado is an adjective – a word of description, which is applied to the person expressing their gratitude – as in the outdated English *(I am) much obliged*. Another adjective you came across was **inglesa** (*English woman*). The masculine is **inglês** (*English man*).

Diálogo 2 *Dialogue 2*

Sylvia arrives and checks in at the hotel where she will be staying before going to the Ferreira home.

Sylvia	Boa tarde. Sou Sylvia Peters. Tem um apartamento reservado em meu nome?
Recepcionista	Um momento. Como se escreve seu sobrenome?
Sylvia	P-e-t-e-r-s. Peters.
Recepcionista	Ah sim, aqui está. A senhora Peters, de Manchester.
Sylvia	Isso.
Recepcionista	Um apartamento com banheiro para três dias, sim?
Sylvia	Sim.
Recepcionista	É o apartamento número quinze, no primeiro andar. Aqui tem a chave.
Sylvia	Muito obrigada.
Recepcionista	De nada.

boa tarde *hello, good afternoon*	**com** *with*
tem? *do you have?*	**banheiro(o)** *bathroom*
apartamento(o) *hotel room*	**para** *for*
reservado *reserved*	**três** *three*
em meu nome *in my name*	**dias(os)** *days*
um momento *just a second*	**número(o)** *number*
como se escreve? *how do you write it?*	**quinze** *fifteen*
	no primeiro andar *on the first floor*
sobrenome(o) *surname*	**chave(a)** *key*
de *of,from*	**muito obrigada** *thanks very much*
isso *that's it*	**de nada** *don't mention it*

Exercício *Exercise*

Tick **a** or **b** to complete the following statements.

1	Sylvia Peters is from	**a** London	**b** Manchester
2	She's going to stay	**a** 8 days	**b** 3 days
3	Her room no is	**a** 15	**b** 12

Gramática *Grammar*

1 A, An Um/Uma

The Portuguese words for *a(an)* are:

UM (used with masculine words) **um apartamento** *a room*
UMA (used with feminine words) **uma chave** *a key*

With more than one (ie, in the plural), the words become:

UNS (used with masculine plural words)
uns apartamentos *some rooms*
UMAS (used with feminine plural words)
umas chaves *some keys*

2 The O/A

Similarly, Portuguese has four words to convey the English word *the*:

O	*masculine, singular* (ie, just one)	**o apartamento**	*the room*
A	*feminine, singular*	**a chave**	*the key*
OS	*masculine, plural*	**os apartamentos**	*the rooms*
AS	*feminine, plural*	**as chaves**	*the keys*

3 Plural nouns

When you have more than one item (a noun), the basic way to form the plural is to add an **-s**, as in the examples above:

o apartamento	os apartamento**s**
a chave	as chave**s**

Beware of irregularities, which abound in Portuguese, such as **o mês** (*month*) **os meses** (*months*).

4 Numbers

Here are the numbers 1–20, some of which have appeared in the first two dialogues.

0	zero	**11**	onze
1	um, uma	**12**	doze
2	dois, duas	**13**	treze
3	três	**14**	catorze
4	quatro	**15**	quinze
5	cinco	**16**	dezesseis
6	seis	**17**	dezessete
7	sete	**18**	dezoito
8	oito	**19**	dezenove
9	nove	**20**	vinte
10	dez		

Diálogo 3 *Dialogue 3*

Sylvia pops out in the evening to meet up with the Ferreiras. She knows José but has not yet met Mrs Ferreira.

José Boa noite Sylvia, tudo bem?
Sylvia Oi José, tudo bem.
José Sylvia, esta é minha mulher Marlí.
Sylvia Muito prazer.
Marlí Igualmente. Bem-vinda a São Paulo. Como está?
Sylvia Bem obrigada.
José Bom, vamos sentar? Que vão tomar?

boa noite *hello, good evening/night*
tudo bem(?) *things OK(?)*
oi *Hi*
esta (f) *this*
minha mulher *my wife*
muito prazer *pleased to meet you*
igualmente *likewise*
bem-vinda a São Paulo *welcome to São Saulo*
bom *right then*
vamos *shall we/let's*
sentar *to sit down*
que vão tomar? *what are you going to have to drink?*

Exercício *Exercise*

Can you fill in the missing words from these statements?

(*a*) _______ noite. Tudo _______?
(*b*) Esta _______ minha mulher.
(*c*) _______ prazer.

Gramática *Grammar*

1 *This* Esta

When identifying people, or things, or when pointing them out, the words for *this* (*these*) are:

ESTE (masculine person/thing) *this* **ESTA** (feminine person/thing) *this*
ESTES (masculine plural) *these* **ESTAS** (feminine plural) *these*
Este apartamento *this room* **Estes apartamentos** *these rooms*
Esta chave *this key* **Estas chaves** *these keys*

2 Possession: my, your, etc.

In the dialogues you were introduced to some of the possessive words: **seu** *your*, **minha** *my*. Here is the full table for *my* and *your*:

	SINGULAR		PLURAL	
	masculine	feminine	masculine	feminine
MY	**meu**	**minha**	**meus**	**minhas**
YOUR	**seu**	**sua**	**seus**	**suas**

The possessive word links to the item being possessed, and NOT the person to whom it belongs; therefore to say *my key*, you need to know that key is a feminine word, then you choose **minha** from the table; **minha chave** = *my key*. Similarly, to say *your rooms*, you need to know that room is a masculine word, and it is in the plural, hence **seus apartamentos**. You will learn more possessives as you progress. Note that sometimes you will hear (or see) the possessive forms as, for example: **A sua chave**; **OS seus apartamentos**; with the appropriate word for *the* going with the possessed item.

(O) meu passaporte *my passport* **(AS) suas chaves** *your keys*

3 Questions, Questions

To ask basic questions in Portuguese, all you have to do is raise your voice in a questioning tone at the end of a statement **Tudo bem** *OK* **Tudo bem?** *OK?*

You can also 'tag' question-phrases on to statements, e.g. **Você é inglesa, não é?** *You're English, aren't you?* **Um apartamento para três dias, sim?** *A room for three days, yes?* The answer to both of these questions is **Sim** *Yes*.

There are also Question-words, known as interrogatives, with which you can begin a question. So far you have met:

Quanto? *How much?* **Como?** *How?* **Que?** *What?*

Sumário *Summary*

bom dia	*hello / good morning / goodbye*
boa tarde	*hello / good afternoon / goodbye*
boa noite	*hello / good evening / goodnight*
oi	*hi / hello*
tudo bem?	*how are things?*
como está?	*how are you?*
tudo bem	*fine*
bem obrigado/a	*well, thanks*
tchau	*see you / bye*
muito prazer	*pleased to meet you*

Dicas culturais *Cultural tips*

- Brazilians are very tactile, open, friendly people, and it is common for them to kiss each other on greeting and saying goodbye. Men often shake hands with each other. Take your cue from their behaviour towards you and those around you.

- Brazilian police at airports, border patrols, and in general, are not to be messed with! Make sure you have all your documentation in order (passport, visa, travel docs, driving licence, addresses of where you are staying). It is not unheard of for police to routinely check your vehicle and, inevitably, find something wrong with it. Often they are looking for a bribe, but you must be very careful here, as some travellers proffering money inside their passport have then been fined for so doing! The best policy, in many cases, is to keep quiet and pay the fine.

Atividades

1 Now see if you can do the following:

(*a*) say *good morning, good afternoon, good evening*
(*b*) say *thank you, goodbye* (casually)
(*c*) say who you are
(*d*) ask if there is a room reserved in your name
(*e*) say *Hi, how are things?*

2 Give your part of the dialogue at the airport.

Inspetor Boa tarde. Seu passaporte por favor.
You (say *here it is*)
Inspetor Você é inglês/inglesa?
You (say *yes I am*)
Inspetor Vai passar quanto tempo aqui?
You (say *eight days*)
Inspetor Muito bem. Tchau.
You (say *goodbye*)

3 Work out the answers to these sums and write them out in words in Portuguese.

(*a*) dois e (and) cinco =
(*b*) oito e seis =
(*c*) dezenove menos (minus) dois =
(*d*) um e dez =
(*e*) vinte menos sete =

4 Look at the Bingo card below, and listen for your numbers being called out on the tape. Cross off any you hear, then write out in words in Portuguese the two you are left with.

12	3	18
6	10	9

5 Look at the pictures and link them to what people are saying.

(*i*) boa noite
(*ii*) bom dia
(*iii*) tchau
(*iv*) muito prazer
(*v*) bao tarde

6 Listen to the dialogue in the hotel, and tick the appropriate answers to the questions.

(*a*)	What is the man's name?	John Harris ☐	John Peters ☐
(*b*)	Where is he from?	London ☐	Liverpool ☐
(*c*)	How long is he staying?	6 months ☐	6 days ☐
(*d*)	What is his room number?	12 ☐	2 ☐

Compreende?
Do you understand?

Look at the following hotel booking-in form, and answer the questions that follow.

HOTEL SÃO LUÍS	
NOME:	Senhor T. Andrews
LUGAR DE ORIGEM:	Londres
Nº DE DIAS:	Seis
TIPO DE APTº:	Com banheiro
Nº DE APTº:	treze

1 Is the guest male or female?
2 They are Italian. True or false?
3 They are staying six days. True or false?
4 What type of room have they got?
5 They are in room no. 12. True or false?

2
VOCE É CASADA?
Are you married?

In this unit you will learn

- how to talk about yourself and your family
- how to talk about your home town
- how to give your address and telephone number

Diálogo 1

Sylvia and the Ferreiras are sitting in a cafe in São Paulo. They are getting to know each other a bit better. The waiter (**o garçom**) brings their order.

Garçom	Vamos ver. Um chope para o senhor Ferreira, um cafezinho para a senhora Ferreira, e um vinho tinto para a senhora.
José	Obrigado
Marlí	Você é de Manchester, não é?
Sylvia	Sim, sou.
Marlí	E como é a cidade de Manchester?
Sylvia	Bem, é grande e muito movimentada.
Marlí	Sylvia, você é casada? Tem filhos?
Sylvia	Sim, tenho dois, um filho e uma filha.
Marlí	Como eles se chamam?

Sylvia Meu filho se chama Robert. Ele tem dezesseis anos e é estudante. Minha filha se chama Clare, tem vinte e três anos e é casada.

Marlí E seu marido? Qual é o nome dele?

Sylvia Meu marido se chama Tony e ele trabalha numa empresa internacional que fabrica produtos químicos. E você, Marlí, trabalha?

Marlí Sim, sou professora de portugûes numa escola de línguas. E você?

Sylvia Eu também trabalho – para uma empresa interessante; sou advogada.

vamos ver *let's see*
um chope *draught lager*
cafezinho(o) *espresso coffee*
vinho tinto(o) *red wine*
como é...? *what's...like?*
cidade(a) *city/town*
grande *large*
movimentado *busy*
casada *married*
filhos(os) *children*
tenho *I have*
filho(o) *son*
filha(a) *daughter*
como eles se chamam? *what are they called?*
se chama *is called*
ele/ela tem...anos *he/she is... yrs old*
vinte e três *23*
estudante(o/a) *student*
marido *husband*
qual é o nome (dele)? *what is (his) name?*
trabalha *work(s)*
numa empresa *in a company*
que *that, which*
fabrica *makes/produces*
produtos químicos *chemicals*
professora(a) *teacher*
português *Portuguese*
numa escola *in a school*
línguas(as) *languages*
trabalho *I work*
internacional *international*
interessante *interesting*
advogada(a) *lawyer*

Verdadeiro ou falso?

Say if these statements are **verdadeiro** or **falso**.

	V	F
(*a*) Sylvia is having beer.		
(*b*) Sylvia has three children.		
(*c*) Sylvia's daughter is married.		
(*d*) Marlí is a maths teacher.		
(*e*) Sylvia is a lawyer.		

Gramática

1 Describing places and people

You met adjectives (describing words) briefly in the first unit. Now let's have a look at them in more detail. Generally speaking, adjectives in Portuguese, unlike in English, go *after* the thing or person they are describing, e.g. **uma empresa internacional** *an international company*. Of course this does not apply if you are talking about something introduced by the verb *to be* e.g **Londres é grande** *London is big.*

The important point to remember is that if you are describing something (or someone) that is feminine, or in the plural, you must make the adjective match it by changing its ending – this is known as 'agreement of the adjective and noun'. Many adjectives end in **-o** (the masculine standard), such as **movimentado**. Look how it changes: **movimentado, movimentada ,movimentados, movimentadas.** So, a busy city is **uma cidade movimentada**, and two busy countries are **dois países movimentados**.

Be on the look-out for irregular -ending words. In the dialogue you had:

grande	grande	grandes	grandes
interessante	interessante	interessantes	interessantes
internacional	internacional	internacionais	internacionais

Here are some adjectives you may want to use to describe your town (*town* = **a cidade** = fem).

pequeno *small*	**lindo/bonito** *pretty*
barulhento *noisy*	**industrial** *industrial*
histórico *historical*	**litoral** *coastal*
sossegado *quiet*	**sujo** *dirty*
cultural *cultural*	**agricultural** *agricultural*

You will meet more adjectives as you progress.

2 Ter *To have*

You have now met various parts of this verb. Here it is in full for you to learn:

(eu) tenho	*I have*	**(nós) temos**	*we have*
(tu) tens*	*you have*		
(ele/ela) tem	*he / she has*	**(eles/elas) têm**	*they have*
(você) tem	*you have*	**(vocês) têm**	*you have* (plural)

*As this form is used in only some parts of Brazil, henceforth we shall concentrate on just four verbal forms. You will hear some Brazilians use **tu** plus the verb for **você**. Whilst being grammatically incorrect, it is neverthless a colloquially recognised usage in some areas.

Note that **Ter** is used when you talk about your age, and not the verb *To be*, e.g *I am 15* = **Tenho 15 anos**.

3 *What's your/their name/s?*

There are different ways to express names in Portuguese. You can say:

Qual é (seu) nome? *What is (your) name?* Or **Como (você) se chama?** *What are (you) called?* Or even **Quem é (você)?** *Who are / is (you)?*

Answers may be: **(meu) nome é...** *(my) name is...* Or **(me) chamo/a...** *(I) am / is called...* Or **sou/é...** *I am / s / he is...*

In the dialogue you were introduced to:

Como eles se chamam? *What are they called?*, and **Qual é o nome dele?** *What is his name?* Both of these are dealt with in following sections.

4 *Verbs – present tense*

In Portuguese, the ending of the verb (the action word) changes according to whoever is carrying out the action (the verb's subject). It is vital to get straight at this point the fact that it does not matter if the person is male or female, but whether they are 1st person (*I, we*), 2nd (*you*) or 3rd (*he, she, it, they*). Many people become confused when first approaching these verb forms, as they have just managed to master the concept of the **o/a** endings for male and female nouns and adjectives. Although these endings also appear on some verbs, they are NOT related to gender. Let's take a verb that you met in the dialogue and see what changes happen to it when we want different people to carry out the action.

You had examples of the verb *To work*: **trabalho** – *I work* and **trabalha** – *he works / you work*.

In Portuguese there are three main groups of verbs, as well as a variety of irregular oddities. The main groups are: Group 1 ending in **AR** – the most common; Group 2 ending in **ER**; Group 3 ending in **IR**. The last two are very similar in endings. With only a few exceptions, all these verbs are formed in the same way:

- First you take off the **-ar** ending and you are left with what is called the stem, e.g **Trabalhar** – **trabalh**.

- Then you add on to this stem the appropriate ending according to whoever is doing the action.

- For **-ar** verbs, the endings you require are as follows :

stem +	
-o	*I*
-a	*he, she, you*
-amos	*we*
-am	*they, you (plural)*

Here are a few examples:

falo	*I speak*	**gostamos**	*we like*
trabalha	*he / she works / you work*	**moram**	*they, you live*

The meanings are sometimes ambiguous, so to make sure you really know who is doing the action, you may need to use the words for *he* (**ele**), *she* (**ela**), or *they* (**eles, elas**).

5 Como eles se chamam? *More verbs!*

Some verbs are not content with changing their endings, but also have a little word accompanying them, as in the above example: **Se**. This word here means *selves*, so the question actually means *what do they call themselves*? These 'self' words are known as 'reflexive pronouns', and they make the verb into a reflexive verb.

The full set you need to know is:

me	*myself*	**nos**	*ourselves*
se	*his / her / yourself*	**se**	*them / yourselves*

You will see that they are placed before the verb. If you were in Portugal or speaking with a Portuguese person, they would usually place them afterwards. If you learnt some Portuguese before starting this course you may discover that in Brazil many of the rules of Grammar are much more flexible than in Portugal.

6 More possessives: *his/her*

To say *his / her* (and the plural *their*), in Portuguese, you should say *the (thing) of him / her / them*, as in the dialogue: **Qual é o nome dele?**/*What is his name? What is the name of him?*

The full forms are:

o/a...dele	*his*	**o/a...dela**	*her*
os/as...dele	*his* (pl)	**os/as...dela**	*her* (pl)
o/a...deles	*their*	**o/a...delas**	*their*
os/as...deles	*their*	**os/as...delas**	*their*
e.g **as chaves deles**	*their keys*	**o nome dela**	*her name*

You will also hear **seu/s (sua/s)**, the same form as *your*, but as this can cause confusion, it's better to use the other forms unless the context is completely unambiguous.

Compare **seu nome** *his / her / your name* and **o nome dele** *his name*.

7 Numa *In a*

Numa is actually two words squashed together (or contracted) for ease of pronunciation. They are: **Em** (*in / on*) + **Uma** (*a, fem*) – **Numa** (*in / on a*), e.g. **numa escola** = *in a school*.

You will also find **num** (em + um), **nuns** (em + uns) and **numas** (em + umas), e.g. **nuns apartamentos** *in some rooms*.

In some written Portuguese the two words appear separated (e.g. **em uma**...) although in practice people run them together when speaking.

8 Ser + *professions*

To talk about your, or other people's professions, you use **Ser** (*to be*) plus the name of the profession, e.g. **sou professora** *I am a teacher*.

Note that there is no equivalent to the English word *a*.

Here is a check list of some professions you may need to use. If yours is not here, your dictionary or teacher should be able to help you.

professor/a	*teacher*	**médico/a**	*doctor*
engenheiro/a	*engineer*	**advogado/a**	*lawyer*
dentista	*dentist*	**recepcionista**	*receptionist*
motorista	*driver*	**gerente**	*manager*
estudante	*student*	**secretário/a**	*secretary*

9 *Languages, nationalities*

So far you have met **inglesa** (*English woman*) and **português** (*Portuguese*). Words of nationality, used also to describe the place of origin of something, are adjectives, and the name of each language is the masculine singular form. Look at the following table for more examples. Portuguese does not use capital letters.

	NATIONALITY				**Language spoken**
	masc. sing	*fem.sing*	*masc.pl*	*fem.pl*	
Brazilian	brasileiro	brasileira	brasileiros	brasileiras	português
Portuguese	português	portuguesa	portugueses	portuguesas	português
English	inglês	inglesa	ingleses	inglesas	inglês
American	americano	americana	americanos	americanas	inglês
Spanish	espanhol	espanhola	espanhois	espanholas	espanhol
Argentinian	argentino	argentina	argentinos	argentinas	espanhol
Chilian	chileno	chilena	chilenos	chilenas	espanhol
French	francês	francesa	franceses	francesas	francês
German	alemão	alemã	alemães	alemãs	alemão
Greek	grego	grega	gregos	gregas	grego

Diálogo 2

José wants to note down some of Sylvia's details so that they can maintain links in the future.

José Qual é seu endereço em Manchester Sylvia?
Sylvia Oitenta e cinco Manor, m-a-n-o-r Road, Manchester, Inglaterra.
José Tem telefone?
Sylvia Sim, o número é 0161 – 236 – 553218, e o número do fax é 0161 – 236 – 553222.
José Está bem. E tem telefone aqui no hotel?
Sylvia Sim, estou no hotel Felix, o número é 678990, e estou no apartamento 15.

o endereço *address*	**telefone(o)** *telephone*
oitenta e cinco *eighty-five*	**no hotel** *in the hotel*
Inglaterra *England*	**estou** *I am*

Verdadeiro ou falso?

Say if these statements are **verdadeiro** or **falso**.

	V	F
(*a*) Sylvia lives at 83 Manor Rd.		
(*b*) She has no phone.		
(*c*) She is in the Felix Hotel.		

Gramática

1 More numbers

Unfortunately, you cannot escape numbers – they surround us in everyday situations – money, time, dates. Here is another set for you to try to start learning.

21	vinte e um/uma	**50**	cinqüenta
22	vinte e dois/duas	**60**	sessenta
23	vinte e três	**70**	setenta
24	vinte e quatro	**80**	oitenta
25	vinte e cinco	**90**	noventa
30	trinta	**100**	cem (cento)
31	trinta e um/uma	**101**	cento e um
40	quarenta		

2 Estar *To be*

To say where you are temporarily, you must use **Estar**, the verb *To be* that describes anything temporary, including location e.g. **Estou no hotel** *I am in the hotel.*

The full set of forms for this verb are:

eu estou	*I am*	**nós estamos**	*we are*
ele/ela está	*he/she is*	**eles/elas estão**	*they are*
você está	*you are*	**vocês estão**	*you are*

3 No hotel *In the hotel*

No is another example of a contracted pair of words, in this case **Em** + **O** (*the*). It means *in the*. You will also find **NA** = em + a, **NOS** = em + os, **NAS** = em + as (**nas cidades** *in the towns*).

You will also discover that the word **DE** (*of*, *from*) contracts in the same way: **do/da/dos/das** e.g. **A chave do hotel** *the key of the hotel* (the hotel's key).

4 *Countries*

Nearly all countries in Portuguese also fall into either a masculine or feminine group.

Here are some examples:

MASCULINE COUNTRIES		FEMININE COUNTRIES	
o Brasil	*Brazil*	**a Inglaterra**	*England*
o Canadá	*Canada*	**a França**	*France*
o México	*Mexico*	**a Alemanha**	*Germany*

o Japão	*Japan*	**a Argentina**	*Argentina*
o Peru	*Peru*	**a Itália**	*Italy*
o Reino Unido	*the UK*	**a China**	*China*
os Estados Unidos	*the USA*	**o Portugal**	*Portugal*

So, to say *I am from England* you would say: **sou da (de + a) Inglaterra**, using the contracted form of **DA**.

Dicas culturais

• When out at a café, Brazilians love to drink their **cafezinho** *little coffee* (strong, dark espresso), or when it's hot the **chopp** – cooled draught national lager, the most well-known being **Antártica**. One of this company's ads for its lager used to have the slogan **estupidamente gelada** *stupidly chilled* – it certainly makes sense when the temperature rises!

When giving someone your telephone number, if there is a six in the number, the Brazilians often say **meia** (*half*), and not **seis**.

Sumário

como é...?	*what's ... like?*
como se chama/m ...?	*what is / are he / she / you / they called?*
qual é o (seu) nome?	*what's (your) name?*
tem...anos	*is ... years old*
qual é seu endereço	*what's your address?*
o número do telefone/fax é...	*the telephone / fax number is...*

Atividades

1 Complete your part of the dialogue. José is trying to find out more about you.

José Você é de Liverpool?
You (say *no, I'm from Birmingham*)

José Como é a cidade de Birmingham?
You (say *it's big and industrial*)
José Tem filhos?
You (say *yes I have one son*)
José Qual é o nome dele?
You (say *he is called David. He is 28 yrs old and is a French teacher*)
José Você trabalha?
You (Say *yes, I work for an International company*)

2 Match up the telephone numbers in digits and Portuguese.

(*a*)	quatro dois um cinco três três	i)	368475
(*b*)	seis seis oito quatro quatro zero	ii)	553311
(*c*)	três meia oito quatro sete cinco	iii)	421533
(*d*)	cinco cinco três três um um	iv)	904621
(*e*)	nove zero quatro meia dois um	v)	668440

3 Listen to someone describing their family, work and town, and tick which pictures apply to the descriptions given.

4 Fill in the gaps with appropriate words for numbers/nouns/ adjectives.

(*a*) Tenho (*5*) chaves (*small*).
(*b*) Sr Ferreira é (*Brazilian*).
(*c*) Sylvia tem três (*interesting*) (*children*).
(*d*) Sou de Paris; é uma cidade (*historical*).
(*e*) Marlí tem (*2*) (*German wines*).

Compreende?

One of Marlí's students has received a letter from a new penfriend. Can you read it and answer the questions on it?

Brasília, 8 de janerio

Olá Maria,

Tudo bem? Eu estou muito bem. Vou te dizer um pouco sobre quem sou. Meu nome é Vania, tenho vinte e dois anos e sou de Brasília.
É uma cidade super-grande e moderna, e muito interessante. Não sou casada. Sou estudante de línguas e também trabalho numa escola secundária, sou secretária.

Tchau,

Vania

vou te dizer um pouco sobre quem sou	*I'm going to tell you a bit about who I am*

1 How old is Vania?
2 What is Brasília like?
3 Is she married?
4 What does she do?
5 Now write a short letter like this about yourself.

(You will find an example in the Key to the exercises, on page 201).

3

ONDE É SUA CIDADE?

Where's your town?

In this unit you will learn

- how to describe where your home town is
- how to describe your belongings and recover lost property
- how to describe what things are made of
- about colours

Diálogo 1

Sylvia goes to the Ferreira's house to arrange her stay there. She chats to the daily help (**a faxineira**), Dona Rita.

Sylvia Bom dia. Sou Sylvia Peters, amiga da senhora Ferreira.
D. Rita Bom dia senhora. Como está?
Sylvia Bem obrigada, e a senhora?
D. Rita Eu estou bem, graças a Deus.
Sylvia Marlí está?
D. Rita Ela já vem da escola. A senhora não é daqui, é?
Sylvia Não, sou inglesa. Sou de Manchester.
D. Rita E como é sua cidade? É uma cidade grande como aqui? Onde é? Perto de Londres?
Sylvia Bom, Manchester é uma cidade interessante e bastante grande, mas não como São Paulo.
D. Rita E sua família mora lá com você?
Sylvia Mora, sim, mas também tenho família no centro da

	Inglaterra, em Birmingham, e também numa cidade pequena ao sul do país, perto de Londres. Manchester não é perto de Londres, mas ao nordeste do país.
D. Rita	Aqui está a senhora Ferreira. Vão pegar suas malas não é?
Sylvia	Sim, vamos para o hotel agora e voltamos para o jantar.

amiga(a) *friend*
estou bem *I'm well*
graças a Deus *thank goodness*
Marlí está? *is Marlí at home?*
ela já vem *she's on her way*
daqui *from here*
como aqui *like here*
bastante grande *quite big*
não como... *not like ...*
mora *live*
lá *there*
onde é *where is?*
com *with*
no centro de *in the centre of*
ao sul de *to the south of*
país(o) *country*
perto de *near to*
pegar *to get/fetch*
malas(as) *suitcases*
vamos *we're going*
agora *now*
voltamos *we'll return*
jantar(o) *dinner*

Verdadeiro ou falso?

Tick true or false for the following statements based on the dialogue.

	T	F
(*a*) Marlí está em casa (*at home*).		
(*b*) Sylvia tem família em Manchester.		
(*c*) Londres é longe de Manchester.		
(*d*) Marlí e Sylvia vão para o hotel.		
(*e*) Elas vão jantar no hotel.		

Gramática

1 *X's friend*

When talking about possession in the 3rd person (he/she/it/they), remember you learnt to say *the (thing) of him / her*, etc. in unit 2. The same applies if you want to use alternatives to him/her, such as *the teacher's key, the student's room,* etc. You must turn the sentence around in Portuguese and say:

the key of the teacher – **a chave do professor (da professora)**
the room of the students – **o apartamento dos estudantes.**

In the dialogue you met **'amiga da senhora Ferreira'** – *Mrs Ferreira's friend.*

2 Mr and Mrs

The expressions for *Mr* and *Mrs* are **(o) senhor** , [**sr**] and **(a) senhora**, [**sra**]. These combine with words such as **de** to form **do sr/da sra**, e.g. **a casa do senhor Villas Boas** *Mr Villa Boas' house.*

3 Locations

If you are describing where your home town or place of work is, the following may be useful:

***ao norte (de)**	*in / to the north (of)*	**ao leste**	*in the east*
ao sul	*in the south*	**ao oeste**	*in the west*
ao/no centro (de)	*in the centre (of)*	**na costa**	*on the coast*
no interior	*inland*	**no litoral**	*on the coast*
perto de	*near*	**longe de**	*far (from)*

***Ao** = **a** (*to / at*) + **o** (*the*). Other contractions involving the word **A** (which is known as a preposition – a locating word) are:

A + A =À
A + OS = AOS
A + AS = ÀS

Try not to be thrown off balance by the fact that the word **A** in Portuguese also means *the* in the feminine form.

Liverpool é ao norte da Inglaterra.	*Liverpool is in the north of England.*
Brasília é no centro do Brasil.	*Brasília is in the centre of Brazil.*
Campinas é no interior de São Paulo.	*Campinas is in the interior of São Paulo (State).*

4 Ir *To go*

You met parts of this important irregular verb in the dialogue: **vão** – *you (pl) are going*, and **vamos** – *we're going* (also meaning *let's…*).

In full, the verb is:

vou	*I'm going / I go*	**vamos**	*we're going / go*
vai	*s / he's going / s / he goes*	**vão**	*they're going / they go*
	you're going / you go		*you're going / you go* (pl.)

Diálogo 2

Sylvia realises she left her bag in the taxi on the way to the Ferreira's. Marlí takes her to the taxi lost property office (**a seção de perdidos e achados**) where she talks to an employee (**empregado**).

Empregado Bom, vamos ver. Uma bolsa, sim?
Sylvia Isso. É bem pequena.
Empregado De que é? De couro, de plástico, de quê?
Sylvia De couro.
Empregado E de que cor é?
Sylvia Preta e roxa.
Empregado E tem alguma coisa dentro?
Sylvia Sim, tem a chave do hotel, uma carteira com dinheiro, minha agenda, e meus óculos de sol amarelos.
Empregado É esta? (shows her a bag)
Sylvia Sim, é. Obrigada. É muito gentil.
Empregado De nada. Faça o favor de assinar aqui. Bom dia.

bolsa(a) *bag*
de que é *what's it (made) of?*
(de) couro *leather*
(de) plástico *plastic*
de que cor é? *what colour is it?*
preto *black*
roxo *purple*
alguma coisa *something*
dentro *inside*
carteira(a) *purse/wallet*
dinheiro(o) *money*
agenda(a) *diary*
óculos de sol(os) *sunglasses*
amarelos *yellow*
gentil *kind*
faça favor de assinar *please sign*

Exercício

Answer **sim** *yes* or **não** *no* to these statements.

(*a*) A bolsa de Sylvia é de couro. ________
(*b*) É preta. ________
(*c*) Tem o passaporte dentro. ________

Gramática

1 De que é (feito)? *What's it made of?*

To describe what something is made from, Portuguese often uses the structure: a (thing) of (material). Look at these examples:

De: **plástico**	*plastic*	**papel**	*paper*
couro	*leather*	**lã**	*wool*
vidro	*glass*	**algodão**	*cotton*
metal	*metal*	**pedra**	*stone*
madeira	*wood*	**tijolo**	*brick / tile*

e.g. **uma bolsa de plástico** *a plastic bag* ***and*** **uma toalha de algodão** *a cotton towel.*

You can of course find examples such as **uma bolsa plástica** and **uma chave metálica**.

2 As cores *Colours*

You will also need to know some colours to describe personal possessions, or even features of people (eyes, etc).

preto *black*	**verde** *green*
branco *white*	**marrom** (pl = **marrons**) *brown*
roxo *purple*	**vermelho** *red*
azul (pl = **azuis**) *blue*	**laranja** *orange*
amarelo *yellow*	**rosa** *pink*
escuro *dark*	**claro** *light*

Remember that colours are adjectives. They must change their endings where appropriate to match the noun(s) they are describing. They also go after the noun. e.g.

uma chave branca	*a white key*
dois passaportes azuis	*two blue passports*
óculos marrons escuros	*dark brown glasses*

3 Faça o favor de *Please*

One of the polite ways of asking people to do things is by using the structure of **faça o favor de + verb**. This is literally *do the favour of ... ing*. You can use it with any verb. To ask more than one person to do something, change **faça** to **façam**. For example, **Façam o favor de trabalhar** *Please work*.

You may also hear another form, **faz o favor de** ..., with an identical meaning when talking to just one person.

4 Ser/Estar – *An overview*

You learnt the formation for these two verbs in the last unit. Let's look more closely at when you should use each one.

SER

Professions	**Sou professora**
Nationality	**É inglesa?**
Permanent location	**É no centro**
Permanent characteristics	**É grande/preto**
Place of origin	**Sou de ...**

ESTAR

Temporary location	**Aqui está**
Temporary condition	**Como está?**
Position	**Está dentro**

5 *Bags and briefcases*

Here are some suggestions for vocab you may need when describing the contents of your bag.

o passaporte	*passport*	**o telefone portátil**	*mobile phone*
uma caneta	*pen*	**um lenço**	*handkerchief*
os comprimidos	*tablets*	**livro de endereços**	*address book*
bilhetes de ...	*tickets for ...*	**um pente**	*comb*
batom	*lipstick*	**isqueiro**	*cigarette lighter*

Sumário

como é sua cidade?	*what's your town like?*
onde é (sua cidade?)	*where is it (your town)?*
... é uma cidade...	*... is a ... town*
é grande/interessante/pequena	*it's big / interesting / small*
ao norte/sul/leste/oeste	*to / in the north / south / east / west*
faça/m o favor de...	*please...*
de que é feito?	*what's it made of?*
é de couro/vidro/lã	*it's made of leather / glass / wool*
de que cor é?	*what colour is it?*
é preto/azul/vermelho	*it's black / blue / red*

Atividades

1 Decide which verb *to be* (**ser/estar**) you should use in each example, and write the correct form of it.

(*a*) José __________ do Brasil.
(*b*) As cidades __________ grandes.

(*c*) Minha chave __________ dentro da bolsa.
(*d*) João tem um filho; ele __________ médico.
(*e*) __________ Angela, __________ americana.

2 Fill in your part of the dialogue, about where you're from.

Sonia Você é de Nova Iorque, não é?
You (say *no, I'm from Brighton*)
Sonia Onde é Brighton?
You (say *it's a small town in the south of England*)
Sonia É perto de Londres?
You (say *yes, it's quite near*)

3 Listen to someone describing their bag and its contents. Tick the relevant pictures below, according to what you hear.

4 Look at the map overleaf and listen to the description of where certain towns are located. See if you can correctly mark on where the towns should be.

1 =
2 =
3 =
4 =
5 =

choose from:

Santos	Uberaba
Piracicaba	
Campinas	Catanduva

Compreende?

Look at the following postcard, and say if the statements below are **verdadeiro** or **falso**.

oi Paulo,

Estou num hotel no centro da Inglaterra. A cidade é pequena, mas é perto de Birmingham que é grande e interessante.

Um beijo da ...
Ana

Paulo R. da Silva
R. Mem Martin, 25
Piracicaba-SP
10325
Brasil

V F

1. **Ana is staying with relatives.**
2. **She is in the Northwest of England.**
3. **The town is not far from Birmingham.**
4. **She thinks Birmingham is boring.**

4
HÁ UMA FARMÁCIA POR AQUI?

Is there a chemist's round here?

In this unit you will learn

- how to ask for and understand basic directions
- how to talk about the weather
- how to understand time
- how to say *there is / there are*

Diálogo 1

Sylvia pops into the city centre (**o centro**). First of all she needs a chemist.

Sylvia	Desculpe. Há uma farmácia por aqui?
Transeunte (passer-by)	Aqui, nesta rua não há, mas há uma na Rua Cabral.
Sylvia	E onde é esta rua?
Transeunte	Bem, você vai por aqui em frente, vira à esquerda naquela esquina, depois você segue em frente mais um pouco, toma a segunda à direita, e a farmácia é aí.
Sylvia	Fica muito longe?
Transeunte	Não, é só dez minutos.
Sylvia	Obrigada.

desculpe *excuse me*
há *there is/are; is/are there?*
farmácia(a) *chemist's*
por aqui *around here*
nesta rua não há *there isn't one in this street*
mas *but*
você: vai/vira/segue/toma *you/go/turn/follow/take*
em frente *in front/ahead*
à esquerda/direita *on the left/right*
mais um pouco *a little more*
a segunda *the second*
é aí *it's there*
fica muito longe? *is it a long way off?*
é só dez minutos *it's only ten minutes*
naquela esquina *on that street corner*

Exercício

Can you answer the following questions based on the dialogue?

	Yes	No
(*a*) Is there a chemist's where Sylvia is?		
(*b*) Does Sylvia have to turn left?		
(*c*) Is the chemist's a long way off?		

Gramática

1 Há?

To ask if there is a particular shop near where you are, you say **há** (*is/are there*) [a shop] **por aqui**? You can also talk about such locations as: **aqui perto/perto daqui** – *near (to) here*, **nesta rua/cidade** – *in this street/town*. If you are lucky, the answer will be: **sim, há** In the dialogue the answer was negative (**não há**), but at least the passer-by helpfully explained where the nearest chemist's was.

To be more specific in your request for information, use: **onde é?** or **onde fica?** – *where is?* or **onde há** – *where is there (a)?* Understanding the directions is another matter!

2 Directions

To begin with you need to know your basic directions:

à esquerda<	**em frente^**	**à direita>**
left	*straight on*	*right*

Then, some basic instructions:

você > vai	*you > go*
vira	*turn*
segue	*carry on*
toma	*take*

And you will finally discover what you're looking for:

e ... **é aí/fica aí/é por aí** – *and... is there / over there*

You may want to check: **fica longe/perto?** – *is it a long way / near?* or **é longe daqui?** – *is it a long way from here?* If you're lucky the answer will be: **é perto!**

You may well make use of expressions such as:

Pode repetir por favor? *Can you repeat that please?* Não compreendo muito bem *I don't understand very well.* Fale mais devagar *Speak more slowly*.

3 nesta, naquela *in this, in that*

These are two more examples of contracted words. **Nesta** comes from **Em + esta** (*this*) (you met the other forms of **esta** in unit 1). **Naquela** comes from **EM + aquela** (*that*). The full forms of *that / those* are:

aquele (m)	**aquela** (f)	**aqueles**	**aquelas**
aquele senhor	*that man*	**aquelas ruas**	*those streets*
naquela rua	*in that street*	**naqueles livros**	*in those books*

4 *1st – 5th*

When requesting directions, you also need to know some ordinal numbers, so that you can turn down the appropriate street. Here are a few to get you going. You will need more of them if you are visiting people who live on the 20th floors of high rise blocks!

1st	**primeiro**	*2nd*	**segundo**	*3rd*	**terceiro**
4th	**quarto**	*5th*	**quinto**		

These are adjectives and as such will change their endings to agree with the noun they are describing, e.g. *the second key* = **a segunda chave**, *the 4th street* = **a quarta rua**.

Diálogo 2

Sylvia now needs to find a bank.

Sylvia	Desculpe. Sabe se há um banco perto daqui?
Transeunte	Sim, há um banco no fim da rua, à direita.
Sylvia	E sabe se está aberto agora?
Transeunte	Que horas são?
Sylvia	São onze e meia.
Transeunte	Então, sim, está aberto. Aqui os bancos abrem das oito e meia da manhã até às três horas da tarde.

sabe se *do you know if*
no fim da rua *at the end of the street*
está aberto *is open*
que horas são? *what time is it?*
são onze e meia *it's 11.30*
então *well then*
os bancos abrem *the banks open*
das 8 e meia da manhã *from 8.30 in the morning*
até às 3 horas da tarde *until 3 pm*

Verdadeiro ou falso?

Say whether the following are *true* or *false*.

		T	F
(*a*)	Há um banco perto.		
(*b*)	O banco não está aberto.		
(*c*)	Os bancos abrem até às 4 horas da tarde.		

Gramática

1 *Spend, spend, spend!!!*

Here is a check-list of some of the shops and establishments you may need to talk about.

as lojas	*shops*	**o banco**	*bank*
o mercado	*market*	**o correio**	*post office*
o supermercado	*supermarket*	**a farmácia**	*chemist*

o hotel	*hotel*	**o turismo**	*tourist information*
o restaurante	*restaurant*	**a loja de roupas**	*clothes shop*
o café	*café*	**o açougue**	*butchers*

You will find more on shops in unit 7.

2 Time 1

To ask the time you say **Que horas são?** – literally *what hours are they?* Answers will be:

É meio-dia/meia-noite/uma hora – *It's midday/midnight/one o'clock*

Time past the hour is expressed as:

X (horas) e Y (minutos), e.g. **São cinco e vinte** *It's twenty past five*. Quarter and half past are: **X e um quarto/X e meia**.

Time to the hour is expressed as minutes to (**para**) the next hour, e.g. **São dez para às oito** = *it's ten to eight*.

3 Time 2

Opening and closing times: **aberto/a** = *open* and **fechado/a** = *closed*.

People will express shop times as follows: **... abre/fecha (está aberto fechado) DAS ... (horas) até às ... horas.** e.g. **O turismo abre das nove e um quarto até às dez para às cinco** = *The tourist office opens from 9.15 til 4.50*.

This can be qualified with the part of the day in question: **da manhã/da tarde/da noite** – *in the morning/in the afternoon/at night*, e.g. **às três horas da tarde** = *until three in the afternoon*.

Diálogo 3

Sylvia stops at the **quiosque** in the square to buy a newspaper (**um jornal**).

Sylvia Boa tarde. Uma *Folha de São Paulo* por favor.
Vendedora São 2 reais.
Sylvia Que calor não é?
Vendedora Pois é, hoje está muito quente. A senhora não é daqui, é?
Sylvia Não, sou inglesa.
Vendedora Ah, na Inglaterra sempre chove, não é?
Sylvia Chove muito, mas no verão também faz calor. Mas aqui na cidade não venta, e está muito abafado.
Vendedora É sempre assim – ainda pior por causa da poluição aqui. Eu nao agüento estes dias.
Sylvia Nem eu. Bom, tenho de ir. Tchau.

Folha de São Paulo *SP daily paper*	**faz calor** *it's hot*
por favor *please*	**abafado** *stifling/close*
que calor *isn't it hot*	**é sempre assim** *it's always like this*
são ... reais *that's ... reais*	**ainda pior** *even worse*
hoje *today*	**por causa de** *because of*
quente *hot*	**poluição(a)** *pollution*
sempre *always*	**não agüento** *I can't stand*
chove *it rains*	**nem eu** *me neither*
no verão *in the summer*	**tenho de ir** *I have to go*

Exercício

See if you have understood the dialogue. Choose the correct answers from the boxes.

(*a*) How much is the paper? (a) [2 reais] (b) [3 reais]
(*b*) The vendor thinks in England it's always (a) [raining] (b) [windy]
(*c*) One of the contributing factors to the heavy atmosphere is (a) [pollution] (b) [clouds]

Gramática

1 *The weather* O tempo

There are various ways to describe the weather:

VERB		EXPRESSIONS			
fazer	*to do/make*	**faz calor**	*it's hot*	**faz frio**	*it's cold*
estar	*to be*	**está quente**	*it's hot*	**está frio**	*it's cold*
		está abafado	*it's close*		
chover	*to rain*			**chove**	*it rains*
nevar	*to snow*			**neva**	*it snows*

Ser is only used with weather expressions if you are describing a permanent state, such as climate: **É sempre frio no inverno no Canadá** – *It's always cold in winter in Canada.*

Dicas culturais

- Most shops in Brazil open from 8.30 to 6.30. On Saturdays they open until lunchtime, and it is rare to find anything except cafés or large shopping centres open on Sundays.
- The summer months can become quite intolerable heat-wise, especially if you are away from the coast. Remember the seasons in Brazil are the opposite to the northern hemisphere. The hottest time is January – March.
- Brazilian currency is the **Real** (reais). One Real equals approx. 1.2 US dollars. Inflation in Brazil is notorious for its eccentricity, running over 100% and more, although in recent years it has shown signs of steadying.
- Some Brazilian publications are available outside the country and make good reading practice. You could try getting hold of ***Folha de São Paulo***, ***Veja*** (like *Time*), or ***Visão*** (like *The Economist*).

Sumário

há tem um/a ... por aqui?	*is there a ...round here?*
à esquerda/direita	*on the left / right*
fica muito longe/perto?	*is it far / near?*
está aberto/fechado?	*is it open / closed?*
são ... horas	*it's ... o'clock*
abrem das ... até às ...	*they open from ... to ...*
da manhã/tarde/noite	*in the morning / afternoon / evening*
por favor	*please*
está quente/frio	*it's hot / cold*

Atividades

1 Can you do the following?

(*a*) ask is there a butcher's near here
(*b*) ask where there is a post office
(*c*) ask what time it is
(*d*) say it's 2.30pm
(*e*) say in Germany it rains a little

2 Look at the clocks below and match them to the times given.

i) são cinco e meia ii) é meio-dia/meia noite iii) são vinte e cinco para às nove iv) são três e um quarto v) são para às dez um quarto

3 Look at the map (opposite), then read the directions. In each case say where you would end up if you correctly followed the instructions.

Instructions: starting outside your hotel (* on map).

(*a*) Vira à esquerda, toma a segunda rua à direita, e vai em frente. ... fica na esquina.
(*b*) Vai em frente, e ... é ali à direita. É muito perto.
(*c*) Vira à esquerda, segue em frente um pouco, depois toma a primeira à esquerda, e ... é ali em frente.
(*d*) Vai em frente, e segue a rua um pouco. Toma a segunda à esquerda, depois vira à esquerda, e toma a primeira à direita ... é aí em frente.

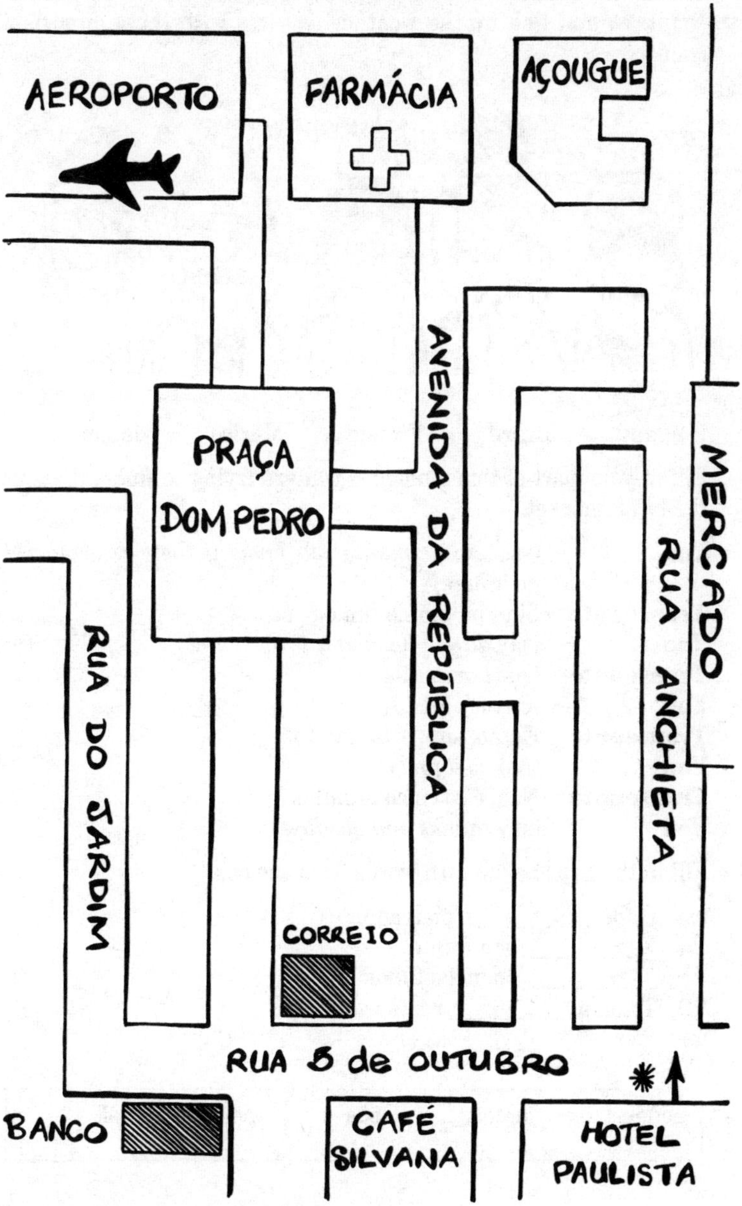
AEROPORTO
FARMÁCIA
AÇOUGUE
AVENIDA DA REPÚBLICA
PRAÇA
DOM PEDRO
MERCADO
RUA ANCHIETA
RUA DO JARDIM
CORREIO
RUA 5 de OUTUBRO
BANCO
CAFÉ
SILVANA
HOTEL
PAULISTA

4 Listen to someone describing the weather today in various countries and link up the weather pictures with the appropriate country.

England Brazil France Mexico Japan

5 Fill in your part of this dialogue. You are trying to find out about the local market.

You	(say *excuse me do you know if there is a market near here*)
Transeunte	Sim, há um no fim da rua
You	(say *do you know if it is open now*)
Transeunte	Que horas são?
You	(Say *it's 10.15*)
Transeunte	Então, sim, está aberto.
You	(Ask *is it far?*)
Transeunte	Não, é só cinco minutos
You	(say *thanks and goodbye*)

6 Fill in the gaps below with words from the box.

(*a*) Onde _________ o mercado?
(*b*) É _________ em frente.
(*c*) _________ são meus filhos.
(*d*) Toma a _________ rua à esquerda.
(*e*) São dez _________ às oito.

aqueles	terceira	fica	para	ali

Compreende?

Read this message that has been left for Sylvia, and answer the questions below.

Sylvia

Pode fazer um favor para mim, e ir ao correio com as cartas?

Vai daqui à esquerda, vira à direita na rua Gomes Sá, e toma a segunda à esquerda que é a rua Nascimento. O correio fica ali em frente. Abre das nove e quinze até às quatro da tarde.

Não é muito longe!

Obrigada

Marlí.

1) Where does Marlí want Sylvia to go?
2) Where should she turn right?
3) Which street on the left should she take?
4) What time does the place close?
5) Is it very far?

5

A QUE HORAS COMEÇA?

What time do you start?

In this unit you will learn

- how to discuss your work
- how to dicuss how you travel to work
- how to talk about daily routine

Diálogo 1

Sylvia and the Ferreiras have gone on a trip to Santos, the most important port on the southern Brazilian coast.

Sylvia Meu Deus! É tão grande – e movimentado. Quantas pessoas trabalham aqui?

José Não sei exatamente, mas deve ser um número enorme. É o porto mais importante do Brasil.

Marlí É mais importante do que Liverpool. Você vê todos os barcos ali? Vêm de toda parte do mundo.

Sylvia Incrível. Marlí, me diga uma coisa – a escola onde você trabalha – tem quantos alunos?

Marlí Tem mais ou menos cento e vinte alunos – dos catorze até aos vinte e cinco anos.

Sylvia Então, é uma escola bastante grande. Você come lá durante o dia?

Marlí Não, a escola não tem refeitório mas eu almoço num café bem perto.

Sylvia A que horas começa?
Marlí Começo às oito e um quarto, tenho uma hora e meia para o almoço, e saio às seis da tarde. Às vezes tenho uma turma à noite.
Sylvia Tanto trabalho!
Marlí É mesmo!

meu Deus! *my god/goodness me*
tão so
quantas pessoas *how many people*
não sei exatamente *I don't know exactly*
deve ser *it must be*
enorme *enormous*
porto(o) *port*
mais importante do/do que *most important in the*
você vê? *can you see?*
todos *all*
barcos(os) *boats*
vêm *come*
toda parte *every part*
mundo(o) *world*
incrível *incredible*
diga uma coisa *tell me*
alunos(os) *pupils*
mais ou menos *more or less*
come *you eat*
durante *during*
refeitório(o) *canteen*
almoço/almoço(o) *I lunch/lunch*
bem perto *really near*
a que horas *at what time*
começa/começo *you/I begin*
saio *I leave/go out*
às vezes *sometimes*
turma(a) *class/group*
tanto trabalho *so much work*
é mesmo *you're right*

Exercício

Choose the correct words to fill in the gaps.

(*a*) Santos é um porto muito _____ grande/pequeno.
(*b*) Marlí come o almoço _____ num restaurante/num café.
(*c*) Marlí trabalha _____ muito/pouco.

Gramática

1 *The most important* O mais importante

When making comparisons between two things, places or people, Portuguese uses **mais de** *more* or **menos de** *less*. The structure is: **X é mais (menos)** *ADJECTIVE* **do que Y**. For example:

Santos é mais importante do que Liverpool.

Often in spoken Portuguese, the **do que** becomes just **que**. The superlative (i.e. the highest degree) of these comparisons is expressed as: **X é o/a _____ mais** *ADJECTIVE*. For example:

Santos é o (porto) mais importante.

Some adjectives have slightly irregular forms of comparison. Look at the table below.

Adjective	Comparative	Superlative
alto *tall*	**mais alto** *taller*	**o mais alto** *the tallest*
grande *big*	**maior** *bigger*	**o maior** *the biggest*
pequeno *small*	**menor** *smaller*	**o menor** *the smallest*
bom *good*	**melhor** *better*	**o melhor** *the best*
mau *bad*	**pior** *worse*	**o pior** *the worst*

Study these examples:

José é mais alto do que Marlí.	*José is taller than Marlí.*
O tempo hoje está melhor.	*The weather today is better.*
Ela é a pior aluna.	*She is the worst pupil.*

2 More verbs

In unit 2 you learnt how to use all the parts of the **-ar** verb **trabalhar**. To talk about daily routines you need to know how to form verbs from the other two main groups.

	-ER	**-IR**
	COMER (*to eat*)	PARTIR (*to leave*)
eu	COMo	PARTo
ele/ela	COMe	PARTe
você	COMe	PARTe
nós	COMemos	PARTimos
eles/elas	COMem	PARTem
vocês	COMem	PARTem

You will see that the endings for these two groups are very similar.

3 Ver, vir *to see, to come*

Irregular verbs are always awkward, and require more concentration in order to learn them adequately. Two verbs most commonly mixed up are **ver** and **vir**. Look at the two of them in the present tense.

VER	VIR
vejo	venho
vê	vem
vemos	vimos
vêem	vêm

4 Todo, todas *All, every*

Todo is an adjective meaning *all/every*, and has four parts agreeing with what it is describing.

todo toda todos todas

You will also come across **tudo**. This is a neuter word meaning *everything/all that*, which is non-specific. It never changes form.

todo (o) dia/todos os dias	*every day*
todas as pessoas	*all the people/everyone*
tudo é bom	*everything is good*

5 *The numbers game 100–1000*

Here are some more numbers for you to learn.

101	cento e um, uma	**190**	cento e noventa
102	cento e dois, duas	**199**	cento e noventa e nove
105	cento e cinco	**200**	duzentos
110	cento e dez	**300**	trezentos
120	cento e vinte	**400**	quatrocentos
130	cento e trinta	**500**	quinhentos
140	cento e quarenta	**600**	seiscentos
150	cento e cinqüenta	**700**	setecentos
160	cento e sessenta	**800**	oitocentos
170	cento e setenta	**900**	novecentos
180	cento e oitenta	**1,000**	mil

6 Time 3

Saying at what time things happen is not much different from what you learnt in the previous unit.

às ____ (horas)	at ____ (o' clock)
às ____ e ____	at ____
às ____ para ____	at ____ to ____
à uma hora	*at one o' clock*
ao meio dia/à meia-noite	*at midday / midnight*

Look at these examples:

às cinco horas	*at five o' clock*
às dez e vinte	*at 10.20*
às quinze para às oito	*at 7.45*

Diálogo 2

José asks Sylvia about her daily routine.

José Sylvia, você mora mesmo em Manchester?
Sylvia Bem, moro a cinco quilômetros de Manchester, numa pequena aldeia, mas trabalho em Manchester.
José Como é que você vai ao trabalho? Vai de carro?
Sylvia Não, de manhã e à tarde o trânsito é impossível, por isso vou de bicicleta no verão. Saio de casa às oito e chego ao trabalho às oito e meia.
José É no inverno – também vai de bicicleta no frio?
Sylvia Não, não tenho coragem – em Manchester chove muito no inverno. Ou vou de ônibus, ou pego uma carona com uma amiga.
José A que horas sai do escritório à tarde?
Sylvia Em geral saio de lá por volta das cinco e meia, mas às vezes fico trabalhando até às seis, seis e um pouco.

mesmo em Manchester *in Manchester itself*
a 5 quilômetros de *5 km from*
aldeia(a) *village*
como vai? *how do you get to?*
de carro/bicicleta/ônibus *by car/bike/bus*
trânsito(o) *traffic*
impossível *impossible*
por isso *for that reason/so*

verão(o) *summer*	**amiga(a)** *friend*
chego *I arrive*	**escritório(o)** *office*
inverno(o) *winter*	**em geral** *generally*
coragem(a) *courage*	**por volta de** *around*
ou ... ou ... *either ... or ...*	**às vezes** *sometimes*
pego carona *I get a lift*	**fico trabalhando** *I stay working*

Exercício

Say if these statements are **verdadeiro** or **falso**.

		V	F
(*a*)	Sylvia lives in Manchester itself.		
(*b*)	In summer she bikes to work.		
(*c*)	Sometimes she works until 9 p.m.		

Gramática

1 ...é que...?/ *...is it that...?*

Often, the expression **é que** (*is it that*) is inserted into a question to either emphasise something important, or simply to enhance the flow of the sentence. If you have studied French, you will recognise the expression *est-ce que*.

2 *Transport*

To talk about means of transport, you use a verb (usually **IR** – *to go*), plus **DE** plus the transport. There are a couple of exceptions. The following table contains more examples.

DE + **carro** *car* **ônibus** *bus* **bicicleta** *bicycle* **ônibus (de luxo)** *coach* **metrô** *underground* **motocicleta** *motorbike* **avião** *aeroplane* **trem** *train* **barco** *boat*
A + **cavalo** *horse* **pé** *foot*

3 *Two irregular verbs* – pedir/sair

These two verbs have certain irregularities, so be careful when using them. In the present tense they are:

PEDIR *to ask for*	**SAIR** *to go out*
peço	saio
pede	sai
pedimos	saimos
pedem	saem

Sumário

é o/a mais... de...	*it's the most... in the...*
é mais/menos ... (de) que...	*it's more / less ... than...*
a que horas começa/termina?	*at what time does it start / finish?*
começo/termino às...	*I start / finish at ...*
ao meio dia/à meia noite	*at midday / midnight*
(você) mora em...?	*do you live in ...?*
como vai ao trabalho?	*how do you get to work?*
vou de carro/bicicleta/táxi	*I go by car / bicycle / taxi*
saio por volta das...	*I leave about ... o'clock*
fico trabalhando até...	*I stay / remain working until...*

Atividades

1 Look at the following extract from Nelson's diary, then listen to him describing his daily routine and fill in the gaps in his diary with activities or times, as though he has written it himself.

8.15	(a)?
8.50	chego ao trabalho
9.00	(b)?
10.00	
(c)?	como o almoço
(d)?	
17.35	
(e)?	chego em casa

2 Fill in the gaps with appropriate times.

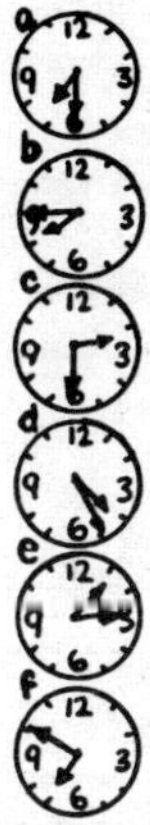

(*a*) Sonia sai de casa _____

(*b*) Miguel vai ao trabalho _____

(*c*) Ana pega o ônibus _____

(*d*) Eu saio da escola _____

(*e*) José come o almoço _____

(*f*) Sylvia chega em casa _____

3 Make sentences describing where places are in relation to each other, writing out in Portuguese the distances.

(*a*) [Germany] **é a** [135 km] **da** [France].
(*b*) [Brazil] **é a** [1896 km] **do** [Mexico].
(*c*) [England] **é a** [1247 km] **de** [Portugal].
(*d*) [USA] **são a** [283 km] **do** [Canada].

4 Match the Questions with the Answers.

(*a*)	Como vai ao trabalho?	i	Mais ou menos 120.
(*b*)	Quantas pessoas trabalham lá?	ii	Ao meio-dia.
(*c*)	Você mora em Londres?	iii	Vou de ônibus.
(*d*)	A que horas come o almoço?	iv	Não, vou a um café.
(*e*)	Você come no escritório?	v	Não, moro em Manchester.

Compreende?

People do all kinds of work. Look at these advertisements overleaf , and see if you can answer these questions.

1) Luci is a fortune-teller. T/F
2) What language must you speak to get the au pair's job?
3) Which advertisement would you answer if you needed some sewing doing?
4) Who can help you if you are suffering from stress?
5) The 26-year-old Brazilian girl would like to be a teacher. T/F
6) Where might you apply for a job if you enjoyed driving?

(*a*)

Gina, massagista terapêutica

KIRODRENAGEM

Trata: celulite, gorduras localizadas, dores, stress.

Atende a domicílio

Para marcar hora ligue 371330

(*b*)

Brasileira

26 anos, 1,56m, falando espanhol, inglês, gostaria de realizar seu grande sonho como atriz, dançarina de samba, lambada, etc.

Favor contatar 0389667

(*c*)

TARÔ &

TRABALHOS ESPIRITUAIS

Se você tem problemas, consulte Luci

484949

(*d*)

Costuras em geral:

Coletas para garçons

Reformas, etc.

6900372

(*e*)

AEROPORTO

- Motoristas profissionais
- Carros novos e confortáveis
- Eficiência e pontualidade
- Serviço de classe

A partir de R$ 26

Tel: 1388926

(*f*)

Procura-se AU PAIR

que fale português, para nos ajudar com a casa e o nosso filho de 4 anos.

Fins de semana livres.

Fale com Lucila

568221

6

O QUE FAZ NO SEU TEMPO LIVRE?

What do you do in your free time?

In this unit you will learn

- how to talk about leisure time
- how to discuss what you like doing
- how to talk about leisure facilities and entertainment

Diálogo 1

Sylvia and the Ferreiras discuss their favourite leisure activities.

José Sylvia, o que você faz no seu tempo livre?

Sylvia Adoro ler. Durante a semana, quando volto do trabalho, gosto muito de escutar um pouco de música, e ler um bom livro.

José Que tipo de livros prefere?

Sylvia Prefiro os livros policiais, mas também leio muitos jornais.

Marlí E qual é a música de que você gosta mais?

Sylvia Gosto da música latina, mas para relaxar ouço música clássica.

Marlí Vai adorar a música popular brasileira – é ótima para dançar.

Sylvia Vocês, o que fazem nas horas vagas?

José Aos fins de semana costumamos passar tempo no clube – nadando, jogando tênis, relaxando no bar. Pessoalmente gosto de jogar golfe, mas Marlí não gosta.

Marlí É verdade, eu prefiro fazer cooper bem cedo de manhã, e aos domingos pratico ioga.

Sylvia E a televisão? As famosas telenovelas brasileiras?
Marlí Só quando não temos mais nada a fazer.

o que você/s faz/em? *what do you do?*
o tempo livre/horas vagas *free/leisure time*
adoro/gosto *I love/like*
ler *to read*
quando *when*
volto/leio/ouço *I return/read/listen*
ouvir/escutar *hear/listen to*
a música latina/clássica *latin/classical music*
a música popular brasileira *Brazilian pop music*
livro(o) *book*
que tipo de *what kind of*
prefere/prefiro *prefers/I prefer*
policiais *police*
jornais(o) *newspapers*
relaxar/dançar *to relax/dance*
vai adorar *you're going to love*
ótimo/a *great*
aos fins de semana *at weekends*
aos domingos *on Sundays*
costumamos *we usually*
passar tempo *spend time*
clube(o) *social club*
nadando/relaxando *swimming/relaxing*
jogando tênis *playing tennis*
bar(o) *bar*
pessoalmente *personally*
não gosta *does not like*
golfe(o) *golf*
é verdade *it's true*
fazer cooper *jogging*
bem cedo *really early*
pratico ioga *I do yoga*
televisão(a) *TV*
as famosas telenovelas brasileiras *the famous Brazilian soap operas*
mais nada a fazer *nothing else to do*

Exercício

Say which activities the characters from the dialogue do and don't like doing.

	reading	sports	television	music
(*a*) Marlí				
(*b*) José				
(*c*) Sylvia				

Gramática

1 Activity vocabulary

Here are some words you will find useful in order to discuss leisure activities.

VERBS	**NOUNS**
jogar tênis/futebol/vôlei/golfe *to play tennis / football / volleyball / golf*	**a piscina** *swimming pool*
passear *to go strolling*	**o clube** *social / sport club*
correr/fazer cooper *to run / go jogging*	**o museu** museum
pintar to paint	**o rádio/a TV** radio/TV
ler livros/revistas/jornais *to read books / magazines / newspapers*	**o centro esportivo** *sports centre*
escutar música *listen to music*	**o cinema** *cinema*
nadar *to swim*	**o teatro** *theatre*
	o campo *countryside*

2 Likes/dislikes/preferences

Some important verbs to express your likes and dislikes are: **gostar (de)/ não gostar (de)/adorar/detestar/preferir/gostar mais (de).**

When talking about activities, all these verbs are followed by an infinitive. Be careful with the *I* person of **preferir**: it is **prefiro.** For example:

Adoro jogar golfe.	*I love playing / to play golf.*
Lúcia prefere ver televisão.	*Lucia prefers to watch / watching TV.*
João gosta mais de nadar.	*John likes to swim / swimming most.*

3 Gostar (de)

Gostar is always followed by **DE**, although this does not add anything useful to the meaning. If the verb is used with a noun, you must remember to combine the **de** with words like **o/a/um**, **uma** etc. if appropriate. For example:

Qual é a música de que gosta?	*Which music do you like?*
Gosto do sol.	*I like the sun.*
Ele gosta mais da cerveja.	*He likes the beer most.*

4 Irregular plurals

Nouns and adjectives which end in **-l** in the singular, have irregular endings, as you saw in the dialogue:

o jornal – jornaIS
policial – policiaIS

Be on the look-out for others as you develop your reading skills.

5 Fazer, ler, ouvir

Some more important verbs with irregularities.

Fazer – *to do, make*	**Ler** – *to read*	**Ouvir** – *to hear*
faço	leio	ouço
faz	lê	ouve
fazemos	lemos	ouvimos
fazem	lêem	ouvem

6 *Time routines*

The days of the week are:

segunda-feira *Monday* **terça-feira** *Tuesday* **quarta-feira** *Wednesday*
quinta-feira *Thursday* **sexta-feira** *Friday* **sábado** *Saturday*
domingo *Sunday*

The week days are all feminine, whilst the week-end days are masculine. Often **-feira** is dropped, people referring simply to **segunda** etc. They are abbreviated thus: 2a/ 3a, etc. To say when you do certain activities, you can say:

aos sábados / aos domingos / ao fim de semana	*on Saturdays / Sundays / at the weekend*
às segundas, terças etc.	*on Mondays, Tuesdays, etc.*
todos/as os/as	*every*

7 ando *ing*

The Portuguese equivalent of the *-ing* form of verbs is formed thus: Verb in infinitive minus the ending (**ar/er/ir**) + **ando/endo/indo**. For example:

escutar *to listen (to)* **escut + ando = escutando** *listening to*

Ele prefere ficar em casa escutando música.	*He prefers to stay at home listening to music.*

BUT to say *I like swimming* you must still use the structure mentioned earlier with the verb *to like* – **gostar de/adorar** + infinitive, e.g. **gosto de nadar** *I like swimming / to swim*.

Diálogo 2

The Ferreiras take Sylvia out to a local bar.

José Quer provar uma bebida nacional Sylvia?
Sylvia O que é?
José É caipirinha. Sabe o que é?
Sylvia Não faço ideia
Marlí É uma delícia – feita de cachaça, uma aguardente de cana de açucar, com limão, açucar e água. É um bocado forte.
Sylvia Então, porque não?
José Garçom, por favor.
Garçom Pois não?
José Duas caipirinhas e uma batida de morango.
Garçom Muito bem.
Marlí Sylvia, você vai ao teatro em Manchester?
Sylvia De vez em quando sim. Prefiro ir ao cinema quando surge a oportunidade. Há bons teatros aqui?
Marlí Ah sim, aqui em São Paulo há muitos – cinemas e teatros com todo tipo de peça – comédia/romance/musical – só que em alguns os ingressos são bastante caros.
José Em São Paulo há coisas para todo mundo – cinema, teatro, museu, discoteca, galeria de arte - há de tudo.

quer provar? *do you want to try?*
bebida(a) *drink*
nacional *national*
o que é? *what is it?*
caipirinha(a) *sugar cane/lime drink*
não faço ideia *I've no idea*
uma delicia *delicious*
cachaça, aguardente *firewater*
limão(o) *lime*
água(a) *water*
pois não? *can I help you?*
uma batida de morango *strawberry/wine*
quando surge a oportunidade *when the opportunity arises*
de vez em quando *sometimes*
peça(a) *play*
ingressos(os) *tickets*
caro/s *expensive*
todo mundo *everyone*
discoteca(a) *disco*
há de tudo *there's a bit of everything*

Verdadeiro ou falso?

Are the following sentences true or false? **T** **F**

(*a*) Caipirinha is an alcoholic drink.
(*b*) Sylvia never goes to the theatre.
(*c*) São Paulo has a wide range of activities.

Gramática

1 Querer *to want*

When asking someone if they would like something, you can either say **quer** (lit. *do you want*), or **queria** (*would you like*). Despite the latter being considered more polite in English, it is not considered rude to use **quer**. Here are the two forms in full:

quero	*I want*	**queria**	*I would like*
quer	*you want*	**queria**	*you would like, he, she,* etc.
queremos	*we want*	**queríamos**	*we would like*
querem	*they want*	**queriam**	*they would like*

2 *To know or to know*

There are two verbs for *to know* in Portuguese – **saber** is *to know a fact* or *how to do something*; **conhecer** is *to know a person, place* and *to meet, get to know someone*.

sei	conheço
sabe	conhece
sabemos	conhecemos
sabem	conhecem

e.g. **Que horas são? Não sei.** *What time is it? I don't know.*
Ela conhece meu filho. *She knows my son.*

3 Alguns – *some*

The full version is:

algum	alguma	alguns	algumas

You can also use:

um	uma	uns	umas

Algum, etc. can be contracted with **em** (nalgum) and **de** (dalgum), although you will rarely come across these forms in Brazil.

Study these examples:

Algumas (umas) pessoas trabalham muito.	*Some people work a lot.*
Não gosto de entrar em alguns (nalguns) bares.	*I dont like going in to some bars.*

Dicas culturais

• Many alcoholic drinks in Brazil take as their base the delicious tropical fruits available there. **Batidas** are cocktails of wine, red or white, blended with a fruit – favourites are **batida de coco** (coconut), **morango** (strawberry), **maracujá** (passion fruit), **pêssego** (peach). **Caipirinha** is very potent and easily addictive! The zest of the lime mixed with the firewater, commonly refered to as **pinga** or **cachaça**, means it is extremely easy to drink in copious amounts. Be careful – it has a kick! During the February carnival many people take to the streets with cans filled with pure pinga tied around their necks. No wonder they keep the samba going for five days!

Sumário

o que faz/em no tempo livre /horas vagas?	*what do you do in your free / leisure time?*
gosto muito de ler/escutar música	*I like reading / listening to music a lot*
que prefere?	*what do you prefer?*
prefiro...	*I prefer...*
costumo/costumamos...	*I / we usually...*

aos domingos/às segundas	*on Sundays / Mondays*
você vai ao teatro/cinema?	*do you go to the theatre / cinema?*
de vez em quando/às vezes	*sometimes*
há bons teatros/museus aqui?	*are there any good theatres / museums here?*
há de tudo	*there's a bit of everything*

Atividades

1 Link up the pictures of the activities with what the bubbles are describing.

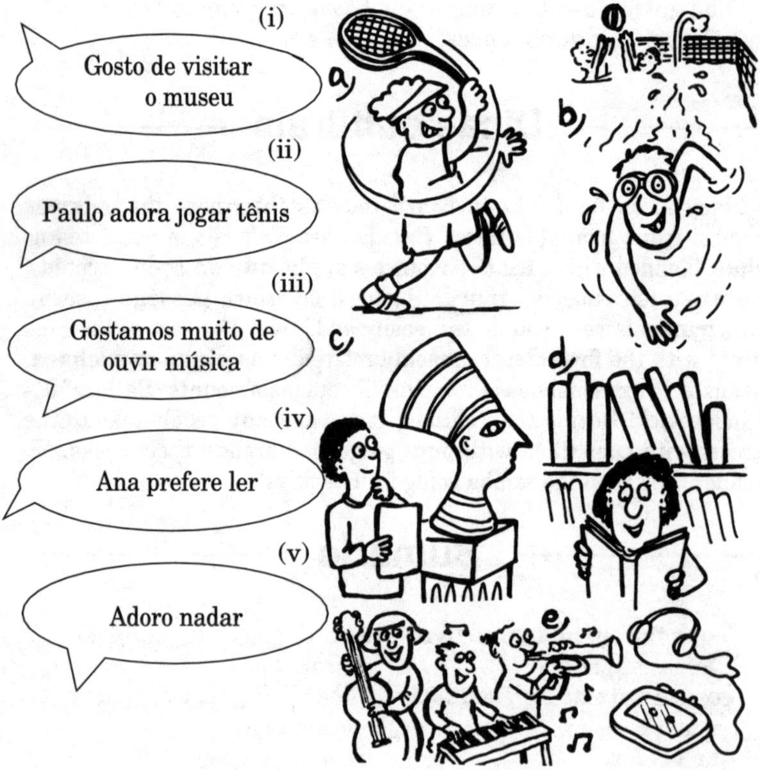

2 **Saber** or **Conhecer?**

Place the correct form of the appropriate verb in the spaces.

(*a*) Eu __________ a França muito bem.
(*b*) Miguel não __________ nadar.
(*c*) A que horas vamos ao cinema? Eu não __________.
(*d*) Sonia, você __________ Senhor Veloso?
(*e*) Eles não __________ esta cidade.

3 Listen to three people discussing what they like doing in their leisure time, and decide which profile below belongs to which person.

(*a*) likes painting, museums and playing golf
(*b*) prefers watching TV, doesn't like sports
(*c*) likes golf and tennis but doesn't like music

Speaker 1= 2= 3=

4 Fill in your part of the dialogue about leisure time.

Francisco O que você faz no seu tempo livre?
You (say *I love swimming, I go to the swimming pool on Saturdays*).
Francisco E você gosta de música?
You (say *yes a little*)
Francisco Que tipo de música prefere?
You (say *I prefer jazz music. Ask Francisco what he does in his free time.*)
Francisco Bom, gosto muito de jogar golfe, e de ir ao teatro.
You (say *I also like the theatre but the tickets are quite expensive.*)

Compreende?

1 Overleaf is some information about courses you can do at a local college. Paulo has chosen a course on Gardening. Look at how he has filled in his subscription form, then choose a course yourself, and fill in the blank form with personal details.

ELECTRÔNICA BÁSICA RADIOTÉCNICA E ÁUDIO TELEVISÃO (P.B. e em Cores)		SILK-SCREEN	GOLFE	ESPANHOL
		DESENHO ARTÍSTICO E PUBLICITÁRIO	VIOLÃO	MECÂNICA DE AUTOMÓVEIS
CORTE E COSTURA	FOTOGRAFIA	ELETRICIDADE	ELETRICIDADE DE AUTOMÓVEIS	AUXILIAR DE ESCRITÓRIO
AUXILIAR DE CONTABILIDADE	AUXILIAR EM ADMINISTRAÇÃO DE EMPRESAS	TRICÔ	BORDADO E CROCHÊ	BELEZA DE MULHER
SECRETARIADO MODERNO	JARDINAGEM	VINHOS	MESTRE DE OBRAS (edificaçôes)	NATAÇÃO
MECÂNICA GERAL	MECÂNICA DE MOTOS	REFRIGERAÇÃO E AR CONDICIONADO	DESENHO DE MECÂNICA	DESENHO ARQUITETÔNICO
ESPECIALIZAÇÃO EM VIDEOCASSETTE	TÉCNICAS DE VENDAS	INFORMÁTICA	INGLÊS	CALIGRAFIA

2 Which courses would you choose if you wanted to study:

(*a*) The guitar
(*b*) General mechanics
(*c*) Art and Design

✂- -

INSTITUTO UNIVERSAL BRASILEIRO SP

Av. Rio Branco, 781 – Caixa Postal 5058 – São Paulo – CEP 01061-970

Sr. Diretor, peço Grátis o folheto sobre o(s) curso(s) profissionalizante(s) livre(s) de Jardinagem ← COURSE

NOME Paulo de Oliveira Martins

RUA Julieta Mesquita **Nº** 35

POST CODE → **CEP** 01326 **BAIRRO** Centro **CX. POSTAL** - ← MAIL BOX No.

CIDADE Belo Horizonte **ESTADO** Minas

↑ DISTRICT

✂- -

INSTITUTO UNIVERSAL BRASILEIRO SP

Av. Rio Branco, 781 – Caixa Postal 5058 – São Paulo – CEP 01061-970

Sr. Diretor, peço Grátis o folheto sobre o(s) curso(s) profissionalizante(s) livre(s) de ______________________

NOME ______________________

RUA ______________________ **Nº** ______

CEP ____________ **BAIRRO** ____________ **CX. POSTAL** ________

CIDADE ____________ **ESTADO** ____________

7

POIS NÃO?

Can I help you?

In this unit you will learn

- how to obtain goods and services
- how to buy clothes and shoes
- how to discuss sizes

Diálogo 1

Sylvia has gone to visit Rio and decides to do some shopping in a fashion store (**a boutique**) before starting her journey northwards.

Empregada Pois não?
Sylvia Queria ver umas camisetas por favor.
Empregada Claro. Qual é seu tamanho?
Sylvia É o 42.
Empregada Você procura uma cor em particular?
Sylvia Tem em verde, ou azul?
Empregada Sim, temos estas aqui, e também aquelas ali em outro estilo. São todas de algodão.
Sylvia Posso provar?
Empregada Claro – a cabine de provas é ali ao fundo.

(Sylvia comes out of the changing room)

Empregada Então, já escolheu?
Sylvia Acho que sim, vou levar esta azul, mas tem a outra em verde-escuro?

Empregada Neste momento não, sinto muito.
Sylvia Não faz mal. Levo as duas. Quanto é?
Empregada São 36 reais ao todo. Quer pagar ali na caixa? Leve este talão consigo. Depois volte aqui para pegar as camisetas.
Sylvia Obrigada.

pois não? *can I help you?*
camisetas(as) *t-shirts*
claro *of course*
tamanho(o) *size*
você procura ...? *are you looking for ...?*
uma cor em particular *a particular colour*
estilo(o) *style*
posso provar? *may I try it on?*
a cabine de provas *changing room*
ao fundo *at the bottom, end*
já escolheu? *have you chosen yet?*
acho que sim *I think so*
vou levar *I'll take*
neste momento *at the moment*
sinto muito *I'm sorry*
não faz mal *that's OK*
quanto é? *how much is it/that?*
ao todo *in all*
pagar *to pay for*
caixa(a) *till/check-out*
leve/volte *take/return*
talão(o) *ticket/stub*
consigo *with you*

Exercício

Only one of these statements is true. Which one?

(*a*) O tamanho da Sylvia é quarenta e quatro.
(*b*) A cabine de provas é à esquerda.
(*c*) Sylvia leva duas camisetas.

Gramática

1 Posso ...?

Posso *may I/can I* can be used with all kinds of verbs in the infinitive, and is very useful. **Posso ver** – *see, have a look* **Posso experimentar, provar** – *to try on, try something, taste* **Posso passar** – *to pass, get by*. The verb is **Poder** – *to be able to* and in full is:

posso	podemos
pode	podem

2 *I think so*

The verb **achar** has various meanings – *to find, think*. It can be used when asking/giving opinions:

Acho que sim/não. – *I think so / not.*
O que você acha? – *What do you think?*
Acho muito bonito. – *I think (it's) very pretty.*

You can also use **creio que** – *I believe* and **penso que** – *I think*.

3 Levo – *I'll take*

Levo is in fact the present tense of the verb even though in English we are saying *I will take* (ie future). This replacement of a future action with a verb in the present tense is very common in Portuguese, especially in spoken dialogue. For example:

Amanhã vejo meu irmão – *Tomorrow I'll see my brother.*
Falamos a semana que vem – *We'll talk next week.*

As in English, you can also use the verb *to go* (**ir**) to express future action. For example:

Vou à cidade amanhã – *I'm going to town tomorrow.*

The future tense will be introduced later in the course.

4 *Commands* – leve/volte

In unit 4, you learnt how to give directions, politely telling people what to do by saying *you (do) this / that*. There are also other ways of ordering people to do things more directly. These are called *commands*, or more technically *imperatives*. Remember that you do not need to be annoyed with someone in order to command them to do or not do something. To form the commands, look at the following steps:

AR verbs	**ER** verbs	**IR** verbs
comprar	comer	partir
(você) compra = *you buy*	**come** = *you eat*	**parte** = *you leave*

To form the command change the verb endings to the following:

comprE! = *buy!* **comA!** = *eat!* **partA!** = *leave!*

There is a crossing-over of endings – the **ar** verbs take an **-e**, and the **er/ir** verbs take an **-a**. To command more than one person, add an **-m**. For example:

(vocês) comprem!	**comam!**	**partam!**

To tell somebody *not* to do something, simply place **não** in front – **não coma!** *don't eat!* Be careful with irregular verbs: here is a small selection of some you have already come across:

fazer	faça!	façam!
ver	veja!	vejam!
ir	vá!	vão!
vir	venha!	venham!
pedir	peça!	peçam!

Be on the look-out for irregular verbs, but don't expect to take verbs on board all at once. They are particularly tricky in Portuguese, and take time to learn.

Diálogo 2

Sylvia next goes to a shoe shop – **a sapataria**.

Sylvia	Bom dia. Queria ver uns sapatos em couro por favor. Tem?
Empregada	Sim, temos. Que número é que você calça?
Sylvia	Acho que é o 38, mas não tenho certeza.
Empregada	Bom, em 38 temos estes, que estão muito na moda agora.
Sylvia	Sim, são muito bonitos, mas queria alguma coisa mais sólida – para andar.
Empregada	Temos estas botas, que são cómodas, e estão em liquidação esta semana.
Sylvia	Posso experimentar?
Empregada	Claro. Tome!
Sylvia	São muito pequenas. Tem outras maiores?
Empregada	Sim, aqui em 39.
Sylvia	Ah sim, estas são mais cómodas. O que você acha?
Empregada	Apesar de ser sólidas, também são 'chique'. Ficam-lhe bem.

Sylvia	Quanto custam?
Empregada	Com o desconto, custam 85 reais.
Sylvia	Que pechincha!

sapatos(os) *shoes*
couro *leather*
tem? *do you have?*
que número...calça? *what size do you take?*
não tenho certeza *I'm not sure*
estar na moda *to be in fashion*
sólido *solid/firm*
andar *to walk*
botas(as) *boots*
cómodas *comfortable*
em liquidação *in the sale*
são muito pequenas *they're too small*
apesar de ser *in spite of being*
chique *chic*
ficam-lhe bem *they suit you*
quanto custa/m *how much does it/they cost?*
desconto(o) *discount*
que pechincha *what a bargain*

Exercício

Answer three questions in Portuguese, based on the dialogue.

(*a*) O que a Sylvia quer comprar? _____
(*b*) Qual é o número das botas que ela compra? _____
(*c*) Quanto custam? _____

Gramática

1 Clothes check-list

a blusa	*blouse*	**a camisa**	*shirt*
as calças	*trousers*	**o vestido**	*dress*
a saia	*skirt*	**a cueca**	*underpants*
a calcinha	*knickers*	**o sutiã**	*bra*
as meias	*socks*	**as sandálias**	*sandals*
as luvas	*gloves*	**o chapéu**	*hat*

2 Materials

algodão	*cotton*	**poliéster**	*polyester*

couro	*leather*	**plástico**	*plastic*
lã	*wool*	**seda**	*silk*
cetim	*satin*	**malha**	*jersey/knitwear*

3 Shops

Often the name of a shop is derived from the item sold there.

sapatos	*shoes*	**sapataria**	*shoeshop*
pão	*bread*	**padaria**	*baker's*
livro	*book*	**livraria**	*bookshop*
pastel	*pastry, cake*	**pastelaria**	*cakeshop*
tabaco	*tobacco*	**tabacaria**	*tobacconist's*
fruto	*fruit*	**frutaria**	*fruitier's*

Sumário

Queria/posso ... ver/ provar/experimentar?	*I woud like to / may I ... see / try on / try?*
Qual tamanho/que número calça?	*What size do you take?*
Em que cor?	*In which colour?*
Tem.../tem em...?	*Do you have / do you have in...?*
Quanto é/quanto custa/m?	*How much is it / does it / they cost?*
Levo/vou levar	*I'll take / I'm going to take.*
Acho que	*I think*
É/são muito pequeno/s, grande/s	*It is / they are too small / large*
Fica/m-lhe bem	*It / they suit you*

Dicas culturais

• Rio is a city of great contrasts. It is arguably one of the most beautiful cities in the world, with its breathtaking scenery and renowned beaches. But there is also great poverty in the shantytowns (**as favelas**). Many will have heard of the police death squads hired by business people to rid the streets of the children who sleep rough. Rio is everything from squalor to extravagance, but it all comes together for its magnificent February carnival – **o carnaval**. Do be careful in Rio – exercise caution when out and about, but don't be too afraid to enjoy its beauty. And don't be shocked by the amount of flesh shown on the beach. Brazilian women don't often sunbathe topless, but their bikinis reveal an awful lot of flesh. Often referred to as 'fio dental' bikinis (dental floss!), they leave little to the imagination. Tone up before you venture on to Copacabana, Ipanema and Leblon!

Atividades

1 Match up the items to be bought with the appropriate shops.

i) livraria	ii) sapataria	iii) mercado	iv) açougue
	v) boutique	vi) padaria	

2 Supply your part of the dialogue in a fashion store

You (Say *do you have skirts?*)
Empregada Sim, temos. Qual é seu tamanho?
You (*Say I think it's 42*)
Empregada Temos estas, em vermelho e preto.
You (Say *do you have it in light-blue?*)
Empregada Sim, temos esta, em outro estilo.
You (Say *how much is it?*)
Empregada Esta custa 46 reais
You (Say *I'll take this one in blue and that one in black.*)
Empregada São 92 reais ao todo.
You (Say *thank you.*)

3 Fill in the gaps by supplying the correct command form of the verb. Then say what each one means.

(*a*) (você) [comprar] _____ a blusa! _____

(*b*) (vocês) [comer] _____ o pão! _____
(*c*) (vocês) [ir] _____ por aqui! _____
(*d*) (você) [não fazer] _____ barulho! _____
(*e*) (você) [trabalhar] _____ bem! _____
(*f*) (vocês) [não falar] _____ muito! _____

4 Listen to someone in a shoe shop, and tick the appropriate pictures for their purchases.

(*a*) Asks for

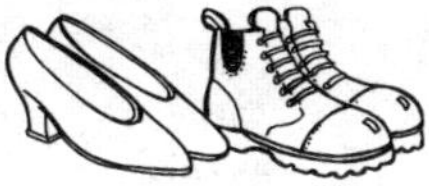

(*b*) Size

(*c*) Colour BLACK BROWN GREEN

(*d*) Do they fit?

(*e*) Price

Compreende?

Look at the advice given to people under their horoscope and answer the following:

1) What should Pisces be eating?
2) What culinary advice is given to Cancer?
3) What should Libra do for their friends?
4) What should Capricorn do on arriving home?
5) What should Aries do before taking a decision?
6) What should Leo treat themselves to?

HORÓSCOPO

PREVISÕES PARA O PERÍODO DE 28 DE DEZEMBRO A 28 DE JANEIRO

CAPRICÓRNIO
22 DEZ. a 20 JAN.
Dica: Quando chegar em casa tome um bom banho de sais.

AQUÁRIO
21 JAN. a 19 FEV.
Dica: Que tal um novo corte de cabelo? Você vai se sentir outra…

PEIXES
20 FEV. a 20 MAR.
Dica: Abuse das saladas. Elas irão manter seu bom humor no verão.

ÁRIES
21 MAR. a 20 ABRIL
Dica: Relaxe muito antes de tomar qualquer decisão.

TOURO
21 ABRIL a 20 MAIO
Dica: Gente. Isso é tudo o que você precisa para melhorar sua vida.

GÊMEOS
21 MAIO a 20 JUNHO
Dica: Não fique apenas pensando em cursos. Faça a matrícula já!

CÂNCER
21 JUNHO a 21 JULHO
Dica: Troque os doces por frutas. Seus dentes vão agradecer.

LEÃO
22 JULHO a 22 AGO.
Dica: Procure uma boa mão oriental e entregue-se às massagens.

VIRGEM
23 AGO. a 22 SET.
Dica: Aposte nos melhores produtos de beleza. Eles vão te ajudar.

LIBRA
23 SET. a 22 OUT.
Dica: Faça um jantar para os seus amigos e ponha um sorriso no rosto, menina.

ESCORPIÃO
23 OUT. a 21 NOV.
Dica: O sol chegou! Aproveite para colocar o bronzeado em dia também.

SAGITÁRIO
22 NOV. a 21 DEZ.
Dica: Viagens à vista. Não tenha medo. Arrume as malas para voar linda.

8

QUE VAI COMER?

What are you going to eat?

In this unit you will learn

- how to order a meal
- more on making requests
- about typical Brazilian food

Diálogo 1

Sylvia goes out to a restaurant with a friend.

Márcia Tem uma mesa livre?
Garçom São quantos?
Márcia Somos só dois.
Garçom Temos esta aqui perto da porta, ou aquela ali ao fundo.
Márcia Esta está bem. Traga o cardápio por favor.
Garçom Tome.
Márcia Deixe ver. O que temos? Há saladas e sopas para começar. Que vai pedir Sylvia?
Sylvia Não tenho muita fome. Quero uma sopa quentinha.
Márcia A canja é boa e típica daqui. É feita de galinha.
Sylvia Então é isto para mim.
Márcia Eu vou pedir uma salada mista para mim.

mesa(a) *table*
livre *free*
são quantos? *how many of you are there?*
somos ... *there are ... of us*
porta(a) *door*
traga *bring*
cardápio(o) *menu*
tome *here you are/take*
deixe ver *let (me) see*
salada/mista *mixed salad*
sopas/sopa quentinha *soups/hot soup*
para começar *to start with*
não tenho muita fome *I'm not very hungry*
canja(a) *chicken broth*
típica daqui *typical of here*
galinha(a) *chicken*
é isto para mim *I'll have this*

Exercício

Say if these statements are **verdadeiro** or **falso**.

	V	F
(*a*) They choose a table near the door.		
(*b*) Sylvia is really hungry.		
(*c*) Márcia chooses soup as a starter.		

Gramática

1 Traga

This command comes from the verb **trazer** *to bring*. In the last unit you were advised to keep a look-out for verbs with irregularities, and here is an example of a verb whose irregularity affects the command-form: **TraGO, traz, trazemos, trazem**. The command becomes **Traga!** *Bring!*

In addition to those listed in unit 7, other verbs which act in the same way include:

Seguir *to follow*	sigo segue seguimos seguem	siga!
Repetir *to repeat*	repito repete repetimos repetem	repita!
Dormir *to sleep*	durmo dorme dormimos dormem	durma!

2 Há

This small word which you met in unit 4 for directions is extremely versatile. It means *there is/there are*, and when used as a question, also means *is there? are there?* It is particularly useful when requesting information about what is available: **o que há?** *what is there?* You can also say **o que tem?** *what do you have?*

3 Ter

The verb **Ter** (*to have*) is used in certain expressions such as **tenho fome** – *I am hungry*.

Ter fome *to be hungry* (literally to *have hunger*).

You will also come across **TER**	**sede**	*to be thirsty*
	sono	*to be sleepy/tired*
	calor	*to be hot*
	frio	*to be cold*

You can also use **ESTAR COM** + **fome**, **sede**, etc.

Diálogo 2

The waiter takes the order.

Garçom Então, já escolheram? Que vão comer?
Sylvia Para começar, uma salada mista e uma canja.
Garçom E depois?
Sylvia Um lombo assado e um filé de peixe frito com batatas fritas, arroz e legumes para dois.
Garçom E para beber?
Sylvia Uma garaffa do vinho da casa.
Garçom Branco ou tinto?
Sylvia Branco. E traga uma jarra de água também por favor – tenho muita sede.
Garçom Muito bem.

já escolheram? *have you* (pl) *chosen yet?*
um lombo assado *roast pork loin*
um filé de peixe frito *fried fish fillet*
batatas fritas *chips*
arroz(o) *rice*
legumes(os) *vegetables*
garrafa(a) *bottle*
o vinho da casa *house wine*
tinto *red (wine)*
jarra(a) *jug*

Exercício

Answer Yes or No

	YES	NO
(*a*) Do they order vegetables for both of them?		
(*b*) Do they ask for red wine?		
(*c*) Is Sylvia thirsty?		

Diálogo 3

The meal continues.

Márcia Garçom por favor!
Garçom Diga.
Márcia Pode trazer mais pão e outra jarra de água por favor?
Garçom Claro. Vão querer sobremesas?
Sylvia O que tem?
Garçom Hoje temos pudim de caramelo, doce de coco, fruta, e sorvete.
Márcia Que sabores de sorvete tem?
Garçom Chocolate, morango, baunilha e avelã.
Márcia Bom, eu quero um sorvete de morango.
Sylvia Eu vou provar o pudim.
Garçom E café?
Márcia Sim, dois cafezinhos.

pode trazer *can you bring*
mais pão *more bread*
sobremesas(as) *desserts*
hoje *today*
pudim de caramelo *creme caramel*
doce de coco *coconut dessert*
fruta *fruit*
sorvete(o) *ice-cream*
sabores(os) *flavours*
chocolate *chocolate*
morango *strawberry*
baunilha *vanilla*
avelã *hazelnut*

Diálogo 4

Paying the bill.

Márcia A conta por favor.
Garçom Aqui está.
Sylvia Quanto é Márcia?
Márcia São 26 reais.
Sylvia Tome aqui.
Márcia Imagine! Pago eu! Insisto. Você é minha convidada.
Sylvia Bom, a próxima vez eu pago. Obrigada. Foi um jantar delicioso. Mas já é tarde. São nove e meia, e amanhã parto para o nordeste.

conta(a) *bill*
pago eu *I'll pay*
insisto *I insist*
minha convidada *my guest*
imagine! *get away/never!*
a próxima vez *next time*
foi un jantar delicioso *it was a delicious dinner*
já é tarde *it's already late*
o nordeste *the northeast*

Sumário

Tem uma mesa livre?	*Do you have a table free?*
Traga o cardápio por favor	*Please bring the menu.*
Que vai pedir/comer?	*What are you going to have/eat?*
O que há/tem? Há/Tem...	*What is there/do you have? There is...*
Tenho fome/sede	*I'm hungry/thirsty*
Para começar/e depois/ para beber	*For starters/and then/to drink*
Pode trazer mais.../outro/a...	*Can you bring more.../another...*
Que sabores?	*What flavours?*
A conta por favor	*The bill please*
Foi um (jantar) delicioso	*It was a delicious (dinner)*

Dicas culturais

• The Brazilians' main staple of food is rice and black beans – **arroz e feijão**, usually eaten with steak – **um filé**, and chips and salad. You can hear the beans cooking away all day in pressure cookers down many residential streets. When eating out, popular choices include Italian food (there is a huge Italian community in and around São Paulo); chicken (**frango**) and fish (**peixes**). Sunday is the day for the infamous black bean stew cooked with all kinds of sausage and off-cuts – **feijoada**. Sometimes it's better not to enquire what every bit is! It is served with rice, **couve à mineira** (sauté green beans) and **farofa** – a bread crumb mixture (**manioc**), and also a slice of orange to aid digestion. In the south you are more likely to eat in a **churrascaria** – **rodízio** – a sort of organised barbecue, where waiters circle the tables with swordsful of every meat you can imagine. As your plate empties you simply catch the waiters' attention. There is usually a help-yourself salad bar, and normally you pay one price and eat until you burst. This is particularly popular in the **gaúcho** – cowboy regions of the south. More about these later in the course.

Meals are leisurely affairs, unless you are working – but even here many a deal has been clinched over an extended lunch.

Typical Brazilian food

Entradas – *starters*

canja	*chicken broth*
creme de aspargos	*asparagus soup*
lula frita	*fried squid*
camarão	*prawns*

Prato principal – *main meal*

lombo assado	*roast pork loin*
frango ensopado	*chicken stew*
ovelha	*lamb*

massa	*pasta*
espeto misto	*mixed kebab*
bife na brasa	*barbecued steak*

Guarnições – *side dishes*

arroz	*rice*
legumes	*vegetables*
batatas fritas	*chips*
farofa	*manioc mixture*

Sobremesas – *desserts*

sorvetes	*ice-cream*
fruta da estação	*fruit of the season*
pudim de caramelo	*creme caramel*
doce de coco	*coconut dessert*

Bebidas – *drinks*

refrigerantes	*soft drinks*
cerveja	*beer*
vinho	*wine*

Atividades

1 Can you do the following?

(*a*) Say *do you have a table free?*
(*b*) Say *there are five of us.*
(*c*) Say *I'm not thirsty.*
(*d*) Ask your friend what they're going to have
(*e*) Call the waiter across
(*f*) Ask for the bill

2 Place an appropriate command from the box below into the spaces.

(*a*) Para o museu? _______ por esta rua!

(*b*) _______ favor!
(*c*) Não _______ todo o vinho!
(*d*) _______ a frase!
(*e*) Não _______ tão rápido!
(*f*) Por favor, _______ mais água!

traga	beba	sigam	coma	falem	faça	repitam

3 Use the food list to help you complete your part of this dialogue.

Garçom Então, já escolheu? Que vai comer?
You (say *to start with a vegetable soup)*
Garçom E depois?
You (say *lamb with rice and salad)*
Garçom E para beber?
You (say *a beer and a jug of water)*
Garçom Muito bem.

4 Listen to the dialogue about desserts and fill in the gaps with the missing words.

A Vão querer _______?
B O que tem?
A _______ temos fruta, _______, e pudim.
B Que sabores de sorvete tem?
A Chocolate, _______, e avelã.
B Bom, eu quero um de _______.
A E café?
B _______ um cafezinho.

5 Fill in the bubbles with the correct form of the verb **ter**, plus the word which describes what the people in the pictures are feeling.

(*a*) Eu...

(*b*) Ana...

(*c*) Nós...

(*d*) Você...?

(*e*) Eles...

6 Look at the various bills from restaurants, and match them to the amounts paid below.

(i)	(i)	(iii)	(iv)
97 Reais	**145 R**	**63 R**	**118 R**

(*a*) sessenta e três reais
(*b*) cento e quarenta e cinco reais
(*c*) noventa e sete reais
(*d*) cento e dezoito reais

7 Indicate where the following food and drink items would appear on a menu, by ticking the appropriate columns.

Item	**starter**	**main meal**	**side dish**	**dessert**	**drink**
(*a*) sorvete					
(*b*) água					
(*c*) café					
(*d*) sopa					
(*e*) bife					
(*f*) legumes					
(*g*) camarão					
(*h*) farofa					

Compreende?

Look at the following menu, then the preference of the people dining out with you. Choose a 3-course meal suitable for all concerned.

Laura is a vegetarian and cannot eat sugar.

Marcelo hates fish/seafood but loves to eat white meat. He loves coconuts.

Sérgio is allergic to shrimps and doesn't like starting a meal with soup. He enjoys eating a mixture of meats in a main meal, and loves very sweet desserts.

You can't manage a starter, but can get through a good steak. You prefer ice-cream for afters.

Rita is very traditional, and likes to start her meal with good, hot broth, followed by fish and likes something fresh for dessert.

	Starter	**Main Meal**	**Dessert**
Laura			
Marcelo			
Sérgio			
You			
Rita			

9
VAI VIAJAR?

Are you going travelling?

In this unit you will learn

- how to travel by various means of transport
- how to ask for change
- how to find out departure and arrival times

Diálogo 1

Sylvia decides to travel northwards to the cities of Salvador and Fortaleza in the **nordeste**. She needs a taxi to get to the coach station. Listen to her conversation at the taxi rank (**o ponto de táxi**).

Sylvia Pode me levar à estação rodoviária por favor?
Motorista Posso, sim, sem problema. Vai viajar?
Sylvia Sim, vou para o nordeste, passar uns dias em Salvador e Fortaleza.
Motorista Cidades bonitas. Também precisa visitar a cidade de Olinda, é muito histórica e faz parte de nosso patrimônio.
Sylvia Vou tentar.
Motorista Aqui estamos.
Sylvia Quanto é?
Motorista 16 reais. Boa viagem.

pode/posso *can you/I can*
levar *to take*
estação rodoviária *bus station*
sem problema *no problem*
viajar *to travel*
passar *to spend (time)*
precisa *you need*
faz parte de *it's part of*
nosso patrimônio *our heritage*
tentar *to try*
boa viagem *bon voyage*

Diálogo 2

Sylvia goes to the ticket office (a **bilheteria**) to purchase her coach ticket.

Sylvia A que horas parte o próximo ônibus de luxo para Salvador?
Empregado Parte às dez e quinze.
Sylvia Queria um bilhete para este se faz favor.
Empregado De ida ou de ida e volta?
Sylvia Só de ida.
Empregado Muito bem. Agora, são 68 reais.
Sylvia Tem troco para uma nota de cem reais?
Empregado Sim, tenho. Tome.
Sylvia Obrigada. O ônibus sai de onde?
Empregado Sai do portão número 22. É por ali à esquerda.

o próximo *the next*
bilhete(o) *ticket*
de ida/de ida e volta *single/return*
tem troco para? *do you have change for?*
uma nota de *a...note*
sai de onde? *where does it leave from?*
o portão número 22 *gate no 22*

Gramática

1 Pode me levar

In unit 1 you learnt the Portuguese words known as personal pronouns for *I*, *you*, *he*, etc. used as subjects of verbs. In the dialogue above, you were introduced to another pronoun, this time an object of the verb, ie the action is done directly to it. In English these *direct object pronouns* are: me, you, him, us, them. In Portuguese they are:

me	*me*	**nos**	*us*
te	*you*	**os**	*them, you* pl.
o	*him, you, it*	**as**	*them, you* pl.
a	*her, you, it*		

In English you may have examples such as *I can see YOU*, *you write IT quickly*, *they hit US*, etc. Usually, in standard written Portuguese, these object pronouns are placed *after* the verb and attached to it by a hyphen (except in certain situations, e.g. negatives, or questions). However, the Brazilians tend to place the object pronouns *before* the verb, whether in a positive or negative statement.

Eu o escrevo	*I write it* (eu escrevo-o)
Eles nos batem	*they hit us* (eles batem-nos)
Você não me vê	*you do not see me*

Often Brazilians will use the object **TE** for you, instead of **o/a**, despite these latter being the correct forms corresponding to **você**. Thus: **Eu te vejo** *I see you*, and not **Eu o/a vejo**. In colloquial Portuguese, Brazilians may quite often say things like **eu vejo você** *I see you* which is incorrect, or **eu vejo ele** *I see him* (literally *I see he*).

2 *Our* nosso

Nosso is the remaining possessive for you to learn. Here is a reminder of the full table of possessives.

	ms	**fs**	**mpl**	**fpl**
Eu (I)	meu	minha	meus	minhas
Você (You)	seu	sua	seus	suas
Ele (He)	o...dele*	a...dele	os...dele	as...dele
Ela (She)	o...dela*	a...dela	os...dela	as...dela
Nós (We)	nosso	nossa	nossos	nossas
Vocês (You)	seu	sua	seus	suas
Eles/Elas (They)	o...deles /delas*	a...deles /delas	os...deles /delas	as...delas /delas

* If no ambiguity, for all forms of *his/her/their* you can use **seu**, **sua**, etc. Don't forget, you will also come across examples of o **meu/a nossa**, etc. For example:

Nosso amigo	*Our friend*
A casa dele	*His house*
João é o meu amigo; sua casa é grande.	*John is my friend; his house is big.*

3 24-hour clock

When travelling, be aware of times given using the twenty-four hour clock. Providing you know your numbers up to 59, you should be OK. The actual structure is a simple adding process, as you learnt in units 5 and 6.

Às dez e quinze	At 10:15
Às treze e trinta e seis	At 13:36
Às vinte e duas e quarenta e cinco	At 22:45

Diálogo 3

Having arrived in Salvador, Sylvia needs to get to the centre.

Sylvia Desculpe senhor. O que faço para chegar ao centro da cidade?
Sr Você vai para onde exatamente?
Sylvia Não sei muito bem. Ao centro.
Sr Bem, tome o ônibus número 5A, que parte daqui, da frente da estação rodoviária, e sai na praça Vicente, que é bem no centro da cidade.
Sylvia Obrigada. O senhor conhece um bom hotel aqui?
Sr Sim, o hotel Beira-mar é muito bom, e não é nada caro.
Sylvia Onde é este hotel?
Sr É na rua Jorge Amado, número 35.
Sylvia Muito obrigada.
Sr De nada.

o que faço para... *what do I do in order to...*
exatamente *exactly*
da frente de *from in front of*
é bem *it's right...*
não é nada caro *It's not at all dear*

Gramática

1 How do I... ?

In the dialogue, this expression was translated as **o que faço para?** (*what do I do in order to?*). You may also come across:

como se faz para...?	*how does one...?*
como posso...?	*how can I...?*

2 In front of – Prepositions

Prepositions – words of place, location, position are varied in Portuguese. You met some in unit 3 which you may like to revise. Here are some more you will find useful when discovering where things are:

em frente (de)	*in front (of)*
detrás/atrás (de)	*behind*
debaixo (de)	*under*
dentro (de)	*inside*
entre	*between*
ao lado (de)	*next to*
perto (de)	*near (to)*
em cima (de)	*on top (of)*
fora (de)	*outside*
contra	*against*

Don't forget that if you are describing a permanent fixture, e.g. a building, you will use **SER** (*to be*) or **FICAR**, but with temporary or moveable items, **ESTAR**. For example:

O mercado é/fica perto do cinema.	*The market is near the cinema.*
Minha casa é ao lado da praça.	*My house is next to the square.*
O livro está em cima da mesa.	*The book is on top of the table.*

Sumário

pode me levar a ... por favor?	*can you take me to ... please?*
vou passar uns dias em...	*I'm going to spend a few days in...*
precisa visitar...	*you need to visit...*
a que horas parte/chega?	*at what time does it depart / arrive?*
o/a próximo/a trem/ ônibus (de luxo)	*the next train / coach*
queria um bilhete	*I'd like a ticket*
de ida/de ida e volta	*single / return*
tem troco para uma nota de...?	*do you have change for a ... note?*
...sai de onde?	*from where does ... leave?*
o que faço para chegar em...?	*how do I get to...?*

Dicas culturais

Transport in Brazil

- **Taxis** are pretty cheap.
- **O ônibus** gets very squashed in town centres, with crowds hanging off the back – wherever they can get hold. You get on at the back of many buses and have to go through a turnstyle. It's awkward if you have much luggage, but cheap.
- **O ônibus de luxo** is for long-distance travel and inter-urban. Cheap. Some are more comfortable than others. There are frequent stops at roadside eating places, the basic equivalent of motorway stops. Also known as **ônibus-leito**, where your seat expands into a bed.
- **O trem** is cheap but very slow. Most longer travel is preferable by coach. Probably the most infamous is the **trem da morte** – the train of death, which crosses the swamplands of the Patanal into Bolivia.
- *1st / 2nd class* **primeira/segunda classes** – *platform* **a linha** – *station* **a estação**

Atividades

1 Insert the correct possessive word in these sentences. You may have to think first about the sentence structure in some of them.

(*a*) Estes são [*my*] _______ sapatos [*shoes*].
(*b*) Sonia é [*his*] _______ amiga. [careful]
(*c*) [our] _______ casa fica perto do cinema.
(*d*) [their f.] _______ irmãs são americanas.
(*e*) Esta é [*your* sing.] _______ chave?

2 Can you do the following?

(*a*) Say *can you take me to the town centre?*
(*b*) Wish someone a good journey.
(*c*) Ask what time the next coach to Rio departs.
(*d*) Ask if someone has change for a fifty R note.
(*e*) Ask how one gets to the Miraflores Square.
(*f*) Ask someone if they know a good restaurant here.

3 Fill in your part of the dialogue at the bus station, and practise it by listening to the cassette.

You	*(Ask what time does the next coach to Fortaleza depart?)*
Empregado	Parte às vinte e uma e dez.
You	*(say you'd like a return ticket)*
Empregado	Muito bem. São 78 reais.
You	*(Ask if he has change for a 100 R note)*
Empregado	Sim, tenho. Tome.
You	*(Ask where the coach leaves from).*
Empregado	Sai do portão número 11B. É aqui em frente.

4 Match up the Portuguese statements on the left with the corrrect English version on the right.

(*a*)	Eu te conheço	i	They don't hear me
(*b*)	Eles não me ouvem	ii	We buy them
(*c*)	Miguel o escreve devagar	iii	The teacher punishes us
(*d*)	A professora nos castiga	iv	I know you
(*e*)	Nós as compramos	v	Michael writes it slowly

5 The following dialogue in a taxi has become scrambled. Can you put it in the correct order?

(*a*) Sim, vou passar uma semana em Minas.
(*b*) Aqui estamos.
(*c*) Pode me levar à estação por favor?
(*d*) Região bonita. Precisa visitar a cidade de Ouro Preto.
(*e*) Quanto é?
(*f*) Posso, sim senhora. Vai viajar?
(*g*) Vou tentar vai viajar?
(*h*) 17 reais. Obrigado.

Compreende?

Look at the travel information on page 99 and answer T/F to these statements.

1) On Saturdays you can get a Transbrasil flight from São Paulo to Rio at 3pm.
2) Ticket A is a train ticket.
3) Ticket B is an inter-city ticket.
4) Ticket A was for a one-way journey only.
5) You can only use ticket B for one journey.
6) You can get a SP-Rio flight with Bio-Sul on a Sunday.

A)

Empr. Auto Onibus Manoel Rodrigues S/A
Inscr. Est. 194000182 - CGC 44581056/0001-52
Av. Pref. Paulo Novaes, 22 - Tel. 22-0550 Avaré

IDA		VOLTA
☑	Campinas	☐
☐	Americana	☐
☐	Piracicoba	☐
☐	Avaré	☐
☐	Piraju	☐
☑	Ourinhos	☐

№ 000754

Data ____/____/____

Preço Cz$ ________

Está incluído no preço o ISTR de 5% - D.I. 1438/75 - Cód. 151
Mod. ISTR N.º 4
INT/SRF N.º 13 - 1/3/77 - Item 22

Autorização n.º 4542

Serie T20 L20 • 10/86
Auto n.º 7789 DER 1976
Linha Ourinhos Campinas
De 000001 a 001000
2.a Via - Passageiro

... rio novo ltda. r e paulo, 1488 - ins. 194014544 - cgc 48387732/0001-02 - avaré

Cia. União de Seguros Gerais União B de Medeiros, 391 Porto Alegre RS cgc 92682038 N.º da Apólice 0321000711

Seguro cz$ .... Limites: cz$ 5.805.00 morte ou invalidez permanente Cz$ 292.83 Assistência Médica e Despesas Suplementares Cz$ 11.610.00 Diárias Hospitalares.

A Empresa não se responsabiliza pela perda dos carros, quando os Srs. passageiros não os apanharem nos pontos oficiais de partida assim como pelas bagagens transportadas gratuitamente.

B)

CBTU
STU - RJ

SUBURBIOS - RIO

CL

ATENÇÃO:

- Este bilhete é válido para 1 (uma) viagem e será rejeitado se for dobrado, amassado ou molhado.

- Coloque o bilhete com a seta voltada para baixo.

Ponte aérea de São Paulo para o Rio

Cia. Aérea	Horários	Preços (R$)*
Vasp / Varig Transbrasil	Dias úteis 2ª à 5ª feira: 6h45 às 22h 6ª feira: 6h45 às 22h30 a cada 30 minutos Sábado: 7h30 às 22h Domingo: 8h às 22h15	R$ 308,50
RIO-SUL TAM	Dias úteis 6h54 e 18h32 7h19 às 18h11	R$ 308,50

* Tarifa ida/volta com taxa de embarque (adulto). RESERVAS (011): RIO-SUL 240-3044; TAM 5585-1800; demais companhias 534-0241.

REVISION EXERCISES ON UNITS 1–9

In this unit you will have further practice of the grammatical points and vocabulary items from units 1–9. You may wish to revise the Gramática sections before you begin, or use this unit as a progress test. All the answers are in the Key on page 201.

1 Decide which article is required for each noun, and tick the appropriate boxes.

	o	a	os	as
livro				
casa				
filhas				
prato				
jornais				
	um	**uma**	**uns**	**umas**
cidade				
senhores				
ruas				
país				
estação				

2 Supply the correct demonstrative (**este**, **este** or **aquele**) in each case.

(*a*) _______ livro que tenho é francês.
(*b*) De quem é _______ caneta que você tem aí?
(*c*) _______ hotéis ali na praça são muito bons.
(*d*) Gosta d_______ casas aqui?
(*e*) _______ óculos ao lado do seu livro são meus.
(*f*) _______ senhora é minha amiga.

3 Use the correct form of **todo** (**tudo**) etc.

(*a*) _______ é muito interessante aqui.
(*b*) _______ minhas amigas estudam português.
(*c*) Ela não gosta de _______ o filme.
(*d*) Quero comprar _______ a roupa.
(*e*) Nós adoramos _______ neste país.
(*f*) _______ as semanas vou ao cinema.

4 Write out the Portuguese for these numbers.

(*a*) 36
(*b*) 152
(*c*) 500
(*d*) 1,321
(*e*) 5,800
(*f*) 12,654
(*g*) 25,000
(*h*) 100,000
(*i*) 14
(*j*) 95

5 What are these numbers?

(*a*) oitocentos e noventa e nove
(*b*) setecentos e vinte e três
(*c*) quatrocentos e sessenta e oito
(*d*) dois mil, quinhentos e um
(*e*) quatro mil, oitocentos e dois
(*f*) sete mil, quinhentos e cinqüenta e quatro
(*g*) onze mil e cem
(*h*) sessenta e oito mil, trezentos e trinta e seis
(*i*) cento e cinco
(*j*) trezentos e sete

6 Form the present tense correctly.

(*a*) Eles não [comer] _______ carne.
(*b*) Eu [falar] _______ alemão.
(*c*) Você [ir] _______ ao trabalho?
(*d*) Ela não [partir] _______ hoje.
(*e*) Nós [fazer] _______ muito barulho.
(*f*) João [viajar] _______ todos os meses.
(*g*) Vocês não [escrever] _______ muitas cartas.
(*h*) Os senhores [compreender] _______?

7 Decide in each case whether the verb should be **ser**, **estar** or **ficar**, and write the correct form.

(*a*) Ela [   ] francesa.

(*b*) Onde [ ] minha bolsa?
(*c*) O banco [ ] ao lado do museu.
(*d*) As chaves [ ] em cima da mesa.
(*e*) Todas as lojas [ ] muito perto do centro.
(*f*) Eles [ ] engenheiros.
(*g*) O apartamento [ ] no segundo andar.
(*h*) João [ ] meu amigo.

8 Make up whole sentences by selecting an appropriate form of **ter** or **haver** and using a suitable ending.

(*a*) Meu irmão	temos	i)	um bom carro.
(*b*) Na cidade	têm	ii)	quinze anos.
(*c*) Nós	tem	iii)	para beber?
(*d*) O que	há	iv)	meu livro?
(*e*) Não	tem	v)	muitas pessoas.
(*f*) Júlia e Maria	há	vi)	fome.
(*g*) Você	tenho	vii)	lojas interessantes.
(*h*) Na praça	há	viii)	uma casa grande.

In the Key you will find suggested sample answers.

9 Form the correct part of the command in each phrase.

(*a*) Falar [sing.] mais devagar.
(*b*) Comer [sing.] menos.
(*c*) Fechar [sing.] a porta.
(*d*) Não abrir [plur.] as janelas.
(*e*) Beber [plur.] mais água.
(*f*) Não subir [plur.] estas escadas.
(*g*) Começar [sing.] agora.
(*h*) Preencher [sing.] esta ficha.

10 Follow the clues to fill in the crossword on nationalities and countries.

Across:
1 Pessoas dos Estados Unidos.
2 O país dos ingleses.
3 A língua dos espanhois.
4 Rio é no...

Down:
5 Paris é o capital da...
6 Vêm da Alemanha.
7 Da Grécia.
8 País dos italianos.
9 Pessoa da China.
10 Os alemães vêm da...

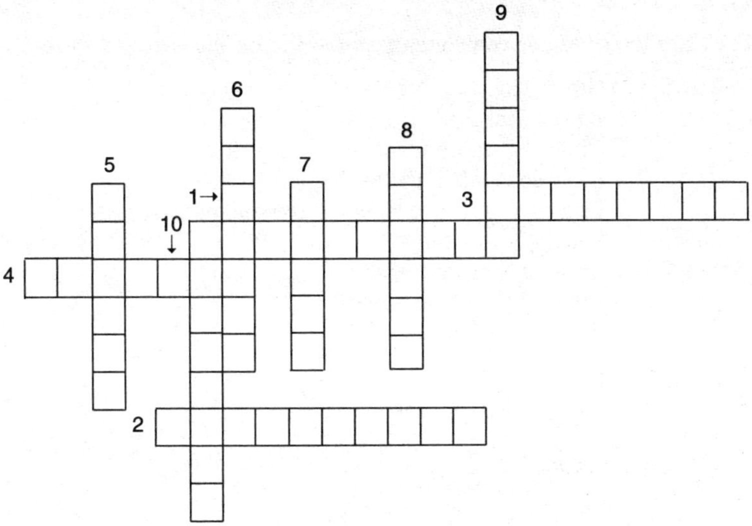

11 Can you complete these words which are all items of clothing?

(*a*) v------
(*b*) s---
(*c*) c--ç-
(*d*) --p-t-
(*e*) --m--a
(*f*) b-u--
(*g*) -h---u
(*h*) l-v--
(*i*) c-s---
(*j*) g----t-

12 Can you find nine colours in this wordsearch?

V	E	R	M	E	L	H	O
E	O	O	T	P	A	M	C
R	L	X	B	C	O	D	N
D	E	O	P	R	E	F	A
E	R	F	R	G	O	H	R
A	A	A	E	B	C	S	B
A	M	Z	T	L	U	Z	A
Q	A	N	O	J	P	T	W

13 Follow the clues and complete the crossword on shops and facilities.

Across:
1 Grande loja.
2 Para trocar dinheiro...
6 Onde se compram botas, sapatos, etc.
7 Onde se vendem frutas, legumes, peixe...
8 Fica na rua – para comprar jornais, mapas, revistas.

Down:
3 Para comprar selos...
4 Onde se compra carne.
5 Onde se compram livros.
8 Para comer e beber...
9 Onde se vê um filme.

10

TEM UM APARTAMENTO LIVRE?

Do you have a room free?

In this unit you will learn

- how to obtain a hotel room
- how to make minor complaints
- more about Brazilian meals and meal times

Diálogo 1

Sylvia approaches the Hotel Florestal in Manaus, Amazon, and enters the reception – **a recepção**.

Recepcionista	Boa tarde. Pois não?
Sylvia	Boa tarde. Tem um apartamento livre?
Recepcionista	Simples ou duplo?
Sylvia	Simples por favor. Com banheiro.
Recepcionista	Todos os apartamentos têm banheiro. Vamos ver. É para quantos dias?
Sylvia	Para cinco dias, até quinta-feira.
Recepcionista	Bom, temos o apartamento 222 livre.
Sylvia	Quanto é por noite?
Recepcionista	58 reais, incluindo o café da manhã.
Sylvia	Está bem. Onde fica o apartamento?
Recepcionista	Fica no segundo andar, com vista para o rio. Quer preencher esta ficha antes de subir?

um apartamento livre *a room free*
simples/duplo *single/double*
para quantos dias? *for how many days?*
por noite *per night*
incluindo *including*
o café da manhã *breakfast*
com vista para o rio *overlooking the river*
preencher *to fill in*
ficha(a) *form*
antes de subir *before going up*

Once in her room Sylvia studies the hotel information guide.

HOTEL FLORESTAL

Tabela de preços:	Quarto só	c/café	meia pensão	pensão completa
apartamento simples	R$40	R$58	R$75	R$95
apartamento duplo (duas camas)	R$35	R$53	R$70	R$90
apartamento duplo (cama de casal)	R$32	R$50	R$67	R$87

Preços por pessoa por noite.

Refeições (servem-se no restaurante *Borboleta*)

café da manhã	a partir das 7:30
almoço	das 12:30 até às 14:00
jantar	das 19:00 até às 21:30

tabela de preços	*price tariff*	**por pessoa**	*per person*
c/café = com café	*with breakfast*	**refeições**	*meals*
quarto	*room*	**se servem**	*are served*
meia pensão	*half -board*	**borboleta(a)**	*butterfly*
pensão completa	*full-board*	**a partir das...**	*from*
duas camas	*2 beds (twin)*	**cama de casal**	*double bed*

Exercício

Can you work out the solutions to the following, based on the above hotel information?

(*a*) Mr and Mrs Johnson would like a twin room, with full board for 2 nights. How much would they pay in total?
(*b*) Are they able to have breakfast served in their room?
(*c*) If they asked to have dinner at 'seis e meia da tarde', would it be available?

Gramática

1 Antes de... *Before ...ing*

To say *before (or after)...ing something*, in Portuguese you use the prepositions **antes de**, *before* or **depois de** *after* plus the infinitive. For example:

antes de subir	*before going up*
depois de descer	*after going down*

You can also use other prepositions in the same way, such as **em vez de** *instead of*, **sem** *without* and **além de** *as well as*.

2 Servem-se

In unit 2 you met reflexive verbs – verbs where the action was carried out on or by a self: **eu me levanto** – *I get myself up*. You can also use reflexive verbs to convey a neutral verb subject, in the same way the French use 'on' (one). **Servem-se refeições** means *meals serve themselves*, ie. *they are served*. This provides an alternative way to saying *we serve* (**servimos**). You may also come across such examples as:

vende-se – *for sale*
fala-se – *is spoken*
compra-se – *is bought*
faz-se – *is made*

Keep a look-out for further examples, especially on signs and in adverts.

Diálogo 2

Sylvia is on her way to look at the grand Opera House in Manaus. At reception she overhears a conversation.

Hóspede (guest) Queria me queixar de algumas coisas de que não estou muito contente.

Recepcionista Qual é o problema senhor?

Hóspede Em primeiro lugar, o ar-condicionado não está funcionando, e com este calor e tantos mosquitos que temos aqui, não agüento ficar no quarto como está agora. Também a torneira da pia não fecha e a água continua pingando toda a noite.

Recepcionista Peço mil desculpas. Vou chamar alguém para vir ver o quarto já já. Está bem?

Hóspede OK, mas também precisa trocar o travesseiro por que está sujo, e dar uma olhada às persianas que não abrem direitinho.

Recepcionista Muito bem senhor. O senhor quer ir jantar enquanto organizo tudo?

queixar-se de *to complain about*
contente *happy*
em primeiro lugar *first of all*
o ar-condicionado *air-conditioning*
não está funcionando *isn't working*
mosquitos(os) *mosquitoes*
como está agora *as it is now*
torneira(a) *tap*
pia(a) *basin*
não fecha *doesn't close*
continua pingando *carries on dripping*
peço mil desculpas *I'm very sorry*
alguém *someone*
já já *right away*
travesseiro(o) *pillow*
sujo *dirty*
dar uma olhada *to have a look*
persianas(as) *blinds*
direitinho *properly*
enquanto *whilst*
organizo *I organise*

Exercício

Name three things wrong with the guest's room.

(1)
(2)
(3)

Gramática

1 Making complaints

In a country as huge as Brazil, it is unfortunately inevitable that something will go wrong at some point. Look at the following check-list of useful expressions:

o aquecimento	*the heating*	**NÃO FUNCIONA/**
a luz	*electricity, light*	**NÃO ESTÁ**
a água	*water*	**FUNCIONANDO**
o ar-condicionado	*air conditioning*	*doesn't work / isn't working*
o chuveiro	*shower*	
a fechadura	*lock*	

a toalha	*towel*	**ESTÁ/ESTÃO**	**sujo**	*dirty*
os copos	*glasses*		**partido**	*broken*
o garfo	*fork*		**lascado**	*chipped*
a faca	*knife*			
a colher	*spoon*			
o prato	*plate*			

falta/faltam – *is / are missing* e.g. **falta um garfo** – *there's a fork missing*

Remember to complain politely! Use **desculpe** to start with, and expressions such as:

pode vir ver	*can you come and look*
pode ajudar	*can you help*
é capaz de	*are you able to*
é possível	*is it possible*

Sumário

tem um apartamento livre?	*do you have a room free?*
simples/duplo	*single / double*
com/sem banheiro/ café da manhã	*with / without bathroom / breakfast*
para ... dias/pessoas	*for ... days / people*
fica no ... andar	*it / s on the ... floor*
queria me queixar de...	*I'd like to complain about...*
o/a ... não está funcionando	*the ... isn't working*
falta/m...	*there's a / some ... missing*
pode dar uma olhada/ajudar/vir?	*can you have a look / help / come?*
peço mil desculpas	*I'm really sorry*

Dicas culturais

• **Apartamento** is the term used in Brazil for an *en-suite room*, otherwise **um quarto** (*room only*) is asked for. Hotels have a different star-rating from what you may have been used to, but you should be able to find something to suit your budget. A **pousada**, unlike in Portugal, is a B&B, although some may be quite pricey. Usually breakfast is included in the price of the room, and certainly worth having – normally a selection of ham, cheese, fruit, cakes and bread rolls. There is a good Youth Hostel service in many parts of Brazil (**os albergues de juventude**), and many motels are also worth considering – however you may be the only ones to still be there in the morning! If you can stand the comings and goings, these are really not a bad deal.

Atividades

1 Take part in a dialogue on the tape about booking a room. Follow the pictures below for your prompts.

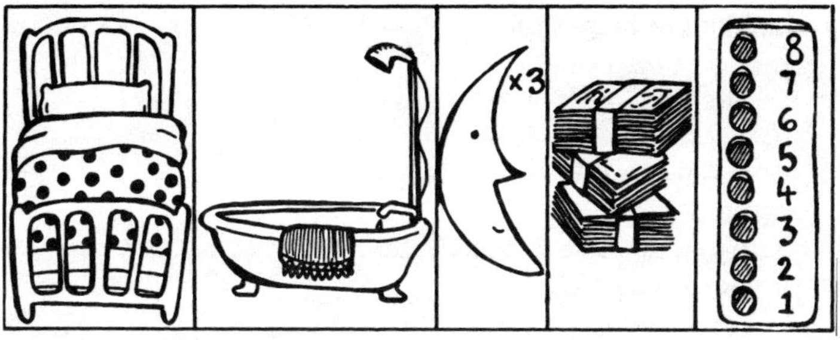

2 Match up the following signs with the pictures.

(i)	(ii)	(iii)	(iv)	(v)
VENDE-SE	FAZEM-SE	COMPRA-SE	FALA-SE	SERVEM-SE

3 Listen to someone booking into a hotel and fill in their details on the **ficha** below.

Room type ------------------------

With/without bathroom --------------------

No. days --------------------------

Departure day ----------------------

Room No. -------------------------

Price per night ----------------------

4 What complaint might you give in each of the following situations?

(*a*) a dirty fork Desculpe ________
(*b*) air conditioning not working
(*c*) dripping tap
(*d*) broken plate
(*e*) spoon missing

5 Choose an appropriate verb from the box to complete the sentences.

(*a*) Antes de _______ à cidade, vou ver minha amiga.
(*b*) Và ao seu quarto sem _______ o jantar!
(*c*) Ana vai viajar depois de _______ o trabalho.
(*d*) O senhor quer sentar antes de _______ o filme?
(*e*) Em vez de _______ água, vou tomar um chá.

IR	TERMINAR	COMER	VER	BEBER

Compreende?

Read the hotel ads and see if you can answer the questions below.

1) If you ring the Itambuca camping, what will you be sent?
2) Which hotels offer free child places?
3) Which ones are near a beach?
4) What do the promotional daily rates include at the Villa Rossa?
5) How many hotels mention they have a swimming pool?
6) In the Villa Rossa luxury 'senior suites' what is the additional costs of R$65 for?
7) Where would you choose if you enjoyed live country music?
8) Which hotel provides you with a colour TV?

Diárias desde R$ 190 incluem as refeições

da Redação

O hotel Villa Rossa tem diárias promocionais a partir de R$ 190, para solteiros em apartamento de luxo nos fundos, e de R$ 215, para acomodações do mesmo tipo para duas pessoas.

Essas diárias incluem pensão completa —café da manhã, almoço e jantar. Uma criança de até dez anos, no apartamento dos pais, tem hospedagem gratuita.

Os apartamentos de luxo que dão de frente para o vale custam, em tarifa promocional, R$ 200 para solteiros e R$ 230 para casais, sempre com as refeições incluídas.

Já os preços da suíte sênior de frente variam de R$ 230 a R$ 250.

Há um custo adicional de R$ 65 para crianças de até dez anos no mesmo apartamento que os pais. Adultos pagam sobrepreço de R$ 85 quando dividem um quarto.

O "check-in" e o "check-out" acontecem às 16h.

A central de reservas do Villa Rossa atende pelos telefones (011) 280-7100 e 280-7495. (SC)

Itamambuca
Pousada & Camping
Planeje suas férias
Sua melhor opção de lazer em Ubatuba
• Junto ao Mar
• Reserva Ecológica
• Piscina
• Quadra de Tenis
• Barcos e Caiaques
• Cantina
• Lanchonete
• Salão de Jogos
• Sala de TV
• Estacionamento
ROD. RIO-SANTOS (BR 101) - Km 36 - UBATUBA - SP
Ligue e receba folheto e
um brinde (012) 445-1175
Praia de Itamambuca

FAZENDA E PRAIA
Hotel Fazenda
Três Poderes
R$ 30,00
C/ PENSÃO COMPLETA
(CAFÉ DA MANHÃ, ALMOÇO E JANTAR)
•Passeio Ecológico a Cavalo e Charrete
•Lago •Piscina Aquecida, Toboágua
•Total Área de Lazer •Animais Diversos
•Apto c/ Frigobar •TV à Cores
ACEITAMOS CONVÊNIOS: Interpass - Mares do Sul - Sisbratur - Candeias
Turisclub - Costa Atlantica - Solemar
CADASTRAMOS AGÊNCIA DE TURISMO
Informações e Reservas: (0124) 27-2411
27-3040

11

QUE TAL ESTA?

What about this one?

In this unit you will learn

- how to further discuss likes and dislikes
- how to express preference
- how to shop for souvenirs
- how to buy snacks

Diálogo 1

Before she leaves Amazônia, Sylvia visits a craft shop to buy some souvenirs.

Sylvia Bom dia. Estou procurando presentes para minha família. Tem alguma coisa típica do Brasil?

Vendedora Temos lembranças muito bonitas aqui – típicas da região, e todas feitas a mão. O artesanato aqui é indígeno, feito pelas tribos do Amazonas.

Sylvia Quanto custa esta bolsa?

Vendedora Esta é de couro e custa 24 reais. Gosta?

Sylvia Sim, adoro, mas tem uma menor? É para minha irmã e ela prefere uma bolsa pequena.

Vendedora Que tal esta? Também é bonita. Ou tem este chaveiro.

Sylvia Prefiro a bolsa. Agora, que tem para homens?

Vendedora Temos cachimbos, carteiras, botas, bengalas...

Sylvia Bom, meu marido detesta fumar, então não vale a

	pena levar cachimbo. Acho que ele vai ficar encantado com uma bengala.
Vendedora	E para si?
Sylvia	Mm, para mim, bem, eu gosto muito de brincos. Tem?
Vendedora	Temos estes feitos de plantas e de plumas – uma recordação linda desta magnífica parte do mundo.
Sylvia	Tem razão. Então levo os brincos, a bolsa e a bengala. Obrigada.

estou procurando *I'm looking for*
presente(o) *gift*
lembranças(as) *souvenirs*
região(a) *region*
feitas a mão *hand-made*
artesanato(o) *handicrafts*
indígeno *indigenous*
tribo(a) *tribe*
o Amazonas *Amazon*
que tal esta? *what about this one?*
chaveiro(o) *key-ring*
para homens *for men*
cachimbo(o) *pipe*
carteiras/bengalas *purses/walking sticks*
fumar *to smoke*
não vale a pena *it's not worth it*
encantado *very happy*
brincos(os) *earrings*
de plantas/plumas *made of plants/feathers*
recordação(a) *reminder*
esta magnífica parte do mundo *this magnificent part of the world*

Gramática

1 Likes, dislikes

In unit 6 you learnt how to use verbs of liking, disliking and preferring, when talking about your favourite leisure activities. In this dialogue you can see how the same verbs are used when referring to objects: **Ela prefere uma bolsa pequena** – *she prefers a small bag*. Be careful with the spelling of **odiar** – *to hate*: **odeio/odeia/odiamos/odeiam** and don't forget **preferir** – **prefiro/prefere/preferimos/preferem**.

2 Para você, para mim

When using the preposition **para** (*for*) with pronouns, you should use the following:

PARA:

mim	nos	
ele	eles	
ela	elas	
si	si	self/selves
você	vocês	

These forms are also used with other prepositions. Look at these examples:

Eu gosto de fazer coisas para eles.	*I like doing things for them.*
Elas fazem tudo para si.	*They do everything for themselves.*
João pensa sempre EM mim.	*John always thinks about me.*

3 Lembranças do Brasil

As you travel around Brazil you will come across varied and exquisite souvenirs. Here are a few suggestions for what to buy:

gaucho-style tea and drinking vessel	**chá erva mate (chimarrão) e cuia (cambuca)**
precious rocks	**pedras preciosas/ouro** (*gold*) **diamante** (*diamond*)
leather goods	**artigos de couro**
earthenware pottery	**cerâmica de barra**
wall hangings	**tapeçarias**
hammocks	**redes**

4 *Souvenir expressions*

Revise shopping expressions, such as:

posso ver/experimentar
gosto mais deste/daquele
tem outro/menor/maior

tem em + *colour*
de que é feito?

Diálogo 2

Sylvia meets a friend for a quick snack before getting ready to leave for Brasília.

Sylvia Oi Paulo. Tudo bem?
Paulo Tudo, e você?
Sylvia Ótimo. Esta viagem é muito interessante para mim. Amanhã parto para Brasília.
Paulo Vai achar Brasília super-diferente – moderna, a sede do governo.
Garçom Que vão tomar?
Sylvia Para mim um café com leite e um lanche.
Garçom De que? Temos hamburguer, cheeseburguer-maionese, coxinhas e empadas.
Sylvia Ai que difícil! Acho que quero uma empada. Paulo o que você vai pedir?
Paulo Para mim, um suco de maracujá, uma coxinha, e um sanduíche de queijo.

esta viagem *this journey*
parto para *I leave for*
vai achar *you'll find*
a sede do governo *the seat of government*
um lanche *snack*
que difícil! *how difficult!*
super-diferente *really different*

Snacks and drinks in Brazilian cafes

Drinks Bebidas

Frias	*cold*	**Quentes**	*hot*
guaraná	*national soft drink*	**chá**	*tea*
vitamina	*milk shake*	**café**	*coffee*
leite	*milk*	**média**	*milky coffee*
suco de fruta	*fruit juice*		
chope	*draft lager*		
laranjada	*orangeade*		

Snacks Lanches

bolo	*cake*
sanduíche de – presunto	*ham sandwich*
queijo	*cheese*
torrada com manteiga	*toast with butter*
coxinha	*chicken 'drumstick'*
empada	*pie*
cheeseburguer/maionese	*cheeseburger / mayonnaise*

Sumário

estou procurando presentes para...	*I'm looking for presents for...*
tem alguma coisa típica?	*do you have anything typical?*
que tal este/esta?	*what about this?*
que tem para...?	*what do you have for...?*
levo...	*I'll take...*
para mim, para meu irmão	*for me, for my brother*
o que vai pedir?	*what are you going to have?*
um sanduíche de queijo/presunto	*a cheese / ham sandwich*
quero um lanche	*I want a snack*
que difícil	*how difficult*

Atividades

1 Complete the sentences by using the correct form of a verb of liking/disliking, plus the appropriate name for the souvenir in the picture.

(*a*) Ela (odiar) ________ a ________.

(*b*) Eu (não gostar) ________dos dos ________.

(*c*) Nós (preferir) _______ a _______.

(*d*) Você (gostar) _______ dos _______?

(*e*) Eles (adorar) _______ os _______.

2 Choose the correct pronouns out of those given.

(*a*) Este bolo é para ME/MIM.
(*b*) Joana não gosta DELES/DOS.
(*c*) Você pensa NELA/NA?
(*d*) Fazem o trabalho para SE/SI.
(*e*) O livro é para VOCÊ/O.

3 Read each person's snack preferences, then choose what each would have.

(*a*)	Sarah wants a hot drink without milk	1) cafezinho 2) média
(b)	Tony is vegetarian	1) sanduíche de presunto 2) torrada
(c)	Sally prefers sweet things	1) bolo 2) coxinha 3) empada
(d)	David wants an alcoholic drink	1) suco 2) chope 3) chá
(e)	Mary hates soft drinks	1) guaraná 2) leite 3) laranjada

4 Take part in a dialogue on the tape, where you are buying souvenirs for your family.

You (Say *I'm looking for presents for my family*)
Sra Temos umas coisas bonitas e típicas do Brasil.
You (Say *do you have a hammock?*)
Sra Temos estas, que são bonitas.
You (Ask *how much it is*)
Sra Esta custa 156 reais.
You (Say *what do you have for ladies*)
Sra Para senhoras temos tapeçarias, pedras, artigos de couro...
You (Say *I'm going to take the hammock, and this wall hanging*)
Sra Obrigada.

Compreende?

Mônica is a 'national heroine' in Brazilian cartoon strips. How much of the text below can you understand?

(1) In how many countries has Mônica already made her presence felt?
(2) When is she going to be launched elsewhere?
(3) In how many other countries?
(4) In the U.S. marketplace, where will Mônica have to be seen to be attending?
(5) In Brazil, what else is the Sousa Prod. C° launching?
(6) What do you think are the words for:
(*a*) little rabbit (*b*) cartoons (*c*) classes.

Mônica vai às aulas

Com o coelhinho na mão, a personagem Mônica ataca outra vez. Presente timidamente em dezessete países, a partir do ano que vem a heroína dos quadrinhos de Maurício de Sousa vai penetrar com força total em quarenta outros, começando pelos Estados Unidos. Para entrar no mercado americano, Mônica terá de freqüentar uma escola. Lá, não se admite faltar às aulas nem nas histórias em quadrinhos. No front interno, a Maurício de Sousa Produções lança o guaraná da Mônica e outros refrigerantes.

12
POR QUE NÃO VAMOS AO TEATRO?

Why don't we go to the theatre?

In this unit you will learn

- how to plan an evening out
- how to get tickets for entertainment
- how to make an invitation
- more time practice

Diálogo 1

Whilst Sylvia is in Brasília she meets up with an old friend Luciane. They are trying to decide what to do later that day.

Luciane Que quer fazer mais tarde?
Sylvia Não me importo. Decida você.
Luciane Que tal o cinema?
Sylvia Se quiser. Que filme está passando?
Luciane Deixe-me ver no jornal. Dê-me aqui. Bom, página 16, aqui está – guia de espetáculos vida noturna. Hmm, no cinema Tivoli está passando 'JFK', no ABC está passando 'Aliens', e no Brasilense 'Wall Street'.
Sylvia Ai Lú, você sabe que não gosto nada destes tipos de filmes.
Luciane Então, fazer, o quê?
Sylvia Por que não vamos ao teatro? Veja o que está passando.
Luciane Bem, tem uma peça satírica no teatro Marisol – é sobre a política no Brasil de hoje em dia. Parece bem recebida pelo público.
Sylvia Ótimo. Vamos lá. A que horas começa?

Luciane Há uma sessão matiné às 3.15 da tarde, e a sessão da noite começa às 7.30. Que horas são agora?

Sylvia São 2.20. Ainda dá tempo para chegar. Vamos de táxi, é mais rápido. Vamos!

mais tarde *later*
não me importo *I'm not bothered*
decida você *you decide*
se quiser *if you like/want*
filme(o) *film*
deixe-me ver *let me see*
guia(o) *guide*
página(a) *page*
não gosto nada de *I don't like at all*
fazer o quê? *do what?*
veja *see!*
peça(a) *play*
satírica *satirical*
sobre *about*
política(a) *politics*
hoje em dia *nowadays*
parece bem recebida *it seems well received*
público(o) *public*
a que horas começa? *what time does it start?*
a sessão matiné *matinee*
ainda dá tempo *there's still time*
rápido *quick*
vamos! *let's go*

Exercício

Can you answer these questions in Portuguese based on the dialogue?

(*a*) Qual é o filme no cinema ABC? ________
(*b*) Os filmes são brasileiros? ________
(*c*) Que tipo de peça há no teatro Marisol? ________
(*d*) Lú e Sylvia vão à sessão da tarde ou da noite? ________
(*e*) Que tipo de transporte elas vão usar? ________

Gramática

1 Dê-me aqui – *more object pronouns*

In the expression **dê me**, what you are actually saying in Portuguese is *give TO ME*. In order to say *to me*, *to you*, etc. you need, unfortunately, another set of object pronouns, called indirect object pronouns. They are:

me	*to me*	**nos**	*to us*
lhe	*to him/her/you*	**lhes**	*to them/you*

****te** (*to you*) is used more frequently than **lhe**.

You use these each time the English has the word *to* in front of the pronoun. You have to be on the look-out, though, because often this is omitted in English. Study this sentence:

Give him the book. If we break it down, we have:

Verb	**Direct object (noun)**	**Indirect object (pronoun)**
give	the book	TO him

In Portuguese this would then be: **lhe dê o livro** (or **dê-lhe o livro**).

You will also hear **dê o livro para ele**. This is often the case in colloquial speech.

2 Pronouns galore!

So far you have met quite a variety of these types of words, and as many people find these small expressions confusing, let's compare them all in a table to help you recognise and learn them.

Subject	Direct Object	Indirect Object	Reflexive
eu	me	me	me
você ele ela	o, a	lhe	se
nós	nos	nos	nos
vocês eles elas	os, as	lhes	se

3 Changes following verbs

With direct object pronouns in the third person (**o**, **a**, **os**, **as**), certain changes occur after verbs which help pronunciation. These changes take place in the following situations:

A) Following verb forms ending in **-r**, **-s**, and **-z**

These final letters are omitted, and an **-l** is added to the beginning of the pronoun. In the case of the omission of final **-r**, the following written accents are added to the remaining final vowel of the verb.

-ar	**-á**
-er	**-ê**
-ir	**-i** (no accent)

Vou vender meu carro	*I'm going to sell my car*
Vou vendê-lo	*I'm going to sell it*

B) Following verb forms ending in **-m**, **-ão**, and **-õe** (nasal sounds)

The endings are maintained, but an **n** is added before the pronoun to preserve the nasal sound.

Eles fazem o bolo	*They make the cake*
Eles fazem-no	*They make it*

Remember that in standard Portuguese usage, object pronouns *usually* follow the verb. However, Brazilian usage is more fluid, and in the spoken language particularly, you will find the pronouns before the verb in many instances.

4 (o) que, o quê, por quê, porque, por que

It can be confusing to come across similar words with the addition, or absence of, written accents, as in the above examples. This is what they mean:

(o) que = *that, which, what*
(o) quê? = *what?*
por quê? = *why?* used on its own, or at end of sentence
porque = *because*
por que? = *why...?*

Look at these examples:

Gosto muito de café. Por quê? Porque é muito saboroso.
O que você vai comprar? Um avião. O quê?
Por que não vai ao cinema? Porque é tarde.
O cinema que eu prefiro é perto de minha casa.

5 Making suggestions

You can use the following expressions:

Que tal...?	*What about?*
Que tal o teatro?	*What about the theatre?*
Que tal a gente* ir ao museu?	*What about us going to the museum?*

***a gente** = colloq. **nós** = *us*

Por que não vai/vamos...?	*Why don't you / we go...?*
Que prefere fazer?	*What do you prefer to do?*
Que quer fazer?	*What do you want to do?*
Vamos...?	*Let's / shall we...?*

Possible replies might include:

ótimo	*great*	**prefiro/preferia**	*I prefer / would prefer*
está bem	*OK*	**quero/queria**	*I want / would like*
OK	*OK*	**boa idéia**	*good idea*
não estou a fim de...	*I don't feel like...*		

6 Describing events

Here are some positive and negative adjectives you may want to use to talk about the cinema, theatre, etc.

É um filme	*film*	**romântico**	*romantic*
uma peça	*play*	**satírico**	*satirical*
um concerto	*concert*	**cômico**	*comical*
uma coleção	*collection*	**triste**	*sad*
uma exposição	*exhibition*	**dramático**	*dramatic*
um show	*show*	**interessante**	*interesting*
		chato	*boring*
		fascinante	*fascinating*
		crítico	*critical*

7 Starting/finishing times

The rules you learnt for time in unit 5 apply to the starting and finishing times of events:

A que horas começa? *What time does it begin?* **Começa às...**
A que horas termina? *What time does it finish?* **Termina às...**
Há um intervalo das...às... *There is an interval from... to...*
de 15 minutos *of 15 minutes*

Diálogo 2

After the play, Sylvia and Lû decide on the rest of the evening.

Sylvia Que boa peça! Foi ótima. Só que não entendi tudo.
Lû Às vezes é difícil – você precisa saber tudo sobre os políticos e a corrupção neste país. Mas gostei.
Sylvia E agora. Que fazemos? Voltamos a pé ou apanhamos um táxi?
Lû Por que não tomamos um copo ali naquele barzinho, e depois vamos jantar naquele restaurante de que você gosta?
Sylvia Mas preciso me preparar para amanhã – vou viajar por Goiânia.
Lû Venha, eu te convido, e sou eu quem pago.
Sylvia Ai, isso não, a gente divide.
Lû Não, insisto. Você é minha convidada aqui e hóspede neste país. Pago eu.
Sylvia Está bem. Aceito. Vamos. E você pode me falar acerca do estado de Goiânia.

foi *it was*
só que *only/just that*
não entendi *I didn't understand*
tudo *everything*
políticos(os) *politicians*
corrupção(a) *corruption*
gostei *I enjoyed (it)*
que fazemos? *what shall we do?*
tomamos um copo *let's have s'thing to drink*
barzinho(o) *small bar*
preparar *to prepare*
venha *come on!*
eu te convido *I'll treat you*
sou eu quem pago *I'll pay*
isso não *no/oh no*
a gente divide *we'll split it*
insisto *I insist*
convidada *guest* (invited)
hóspede (o,a) *guest*
pago eu! *I'll pay*
aceito *I accept*
acerca de *about*
estado(o) *state*

Gramática

1 Foi – *it was, talking about the past*

In the dialogue you were introduced very briefly to ways of talking about the past in Portuguese.

foi *it was* **não entendi** *I didn't understand* **gostei** *I liked*

You will learn the full formations and explanations in unit 15.

2 Barzinho – *small bar*

One way of making things smaller, cuter, more affectionate in Portuguese, is to add **-zinho** (or **-inho**) to the ending of the word in question. Hence:

o bar → o barzinho	*small bar*
o café → o cafezinho	*small coffee*
o livro → o livrinho	*small book / pamphlet*
o gato → o gatinho	*kitten*
obrigado → obrigadinho	*thanks very much*

3 *Particular means of transport*

When specifying a particular vehicle, e.g. a friend's car, or a timetabled bus/train, etc. you use **EM (no/na)** and the vehicle, and not **DE**. For example:

Vou NO carro de José.	*I'm going in José's car.*
Ele vai NO avião da Varig.	*He's going on the Varig plane.*
Vamos NO trem das 2.30.	*We're going on the 2.30 train.*

Sumário

que quer fazer mais tarde?	*what do you want to do later?*
que tal o cinema/o teatro?	*how about the cinema / theatre?*
não me importo	*I don't mind*

se quiser	*if you like / want*
por que não vamos ao museu?	*why don't we go to the museum?*
ainda dá tempo para...	*there's still time to...*
há um filme/uma peça/ um show	*there's a film / play / show*
eu te convido	*it's my turn to pay for you (I invite you)*
sou eu quem pago/pago eu	*I'll pay*
você é meu/minha convidado/a	*you're my guest*

Dicas culturais

• Brazilians love enjoying themselves, and don't need a lot to make them happy. Even a drink in a bar can proceed into a table-patting, match-box shaking accompaniment of a song, and soon the whole place is alive with movement, rhythm and enjoyment. Larger towns and cities are blessed with museums, cinemas, theatres, nightclubs, galleries and plenty of places to eat, drink and soak up the atmosphere. For the more cultured visitor, there are concerts and literary events as well – just look in the local paper or ask at the **Turismo**.

If you don't fancy going out (although you'll miss Brazil if you don't), there are always the amazingly dramatic TV soap operas – the **telenovelas**. Brazilians are hooked on them, some watching three, four or five of them daily! And we thought the Aussie soaps were abundant enough!

Atividades

1 Can you do the following?

(*a*) Suggest to a friend that you go to the museum.
(*b*) Ask at what time the film starts.
(*c*) Say the concert finishes at 10.30pm.
(*d*) Say what a good exhibition.
(*e*) Tell John that he is your guest.
(*f*) Say shall we return by bus.

2 Choose the correct pronouns from those given in the boxes, to fill the gaps.

(*a*) _______ _______ levanto às sete horas.
(*b*) Dá – _______ o bolo!
(*c*) Não _______ importas?
(*d*) _______ vai ao mercado.
(*e*) Vou vendê – _______ à minha amiga.

ME			LHE
	EU	TE	
ELE		LO	

3 Listen to two people discussing how to spend the afternoon, and complete the exercise below by ticking the appropriate boxes, or filling in the missing information:

(*a*)	Marta suggests going to	i) cinema	ii) concert
(*b*)	What page is the info on?	i) 26	ii) 23
(c)	What is Rui's preferred activity?	i) museum	ii) cinema
(*d*)	What is on offer there?	_______	
(*e*)	What time is it?	_______	
(*f*)	How will they get there?	i) bus	ii) walk

4 Fill in your part of the dialogue, inviting a friend out.

Friend E agora. Que fazemos?
You (Say, *why don't we go and have lunch in that little bar over there?*)
Friend Mas preciso me preparar para o trabalho.
You (Say, *come along, I invite you and I'll pay*).
Friend Isso não.
You (Say *I insist – you are my guest*).
Friend Está bem. Aceito.
You (Say, *let's go*).

5 Fill in the gaps with either a *preposition* (**de/a/em**), a *means of transport*, *location*, or *time*, according to the instructions.

(*a*) Vou [prep.] [THE TOWN] [prep.] 

(*b*) Sonia vai viajar [prep.]  [prep.] Varig.

(*c*) Eles vão pegar o  [prep.] 14:00

(*d*) Vamos [prep.] 

? Não, prefiro ir [prep.] 

(*e*) Quer vir [prep.]  [prep.] meu pai?

Compreende?

Read the three film excerpts overleaf, and decide which title belongs with which film?

Now answer the following:

(*a*) Which film is not American?
(*b*) Which film would you choose if you enjoy police stories?
(*c*) Which war does film C relate to?
(*d*) Is film A a comedy or tragedy?
(*e*) How many people are killed in film B?
(*f*) The adaptation for film C is taken from what source?

(i) Brigada de Homicidis

(ii) Nascido a 4 de julho

(iii) Mulheres à beira de um ataque de nervos

(a) Este é talvez o filme mais popular do mais consagrado cineasta espanhol: Pedro Almodovar. Premiado em Berlim com os galardões destinados ao melhor realizador e à melhor atriz (Carmen Maura), o filme é, no fundo, uma grande tragédia, cujas situações levam o espectador a rir até às lágrimas.

(b) O detetive Robert Ross tenta incriminar um perigoso traficante de droga. Mas quando está prestes a deslindar o caso, é-lhe entregue o caso do assassínio de uma velha judia, cujo móbil terá o roubo. Por um lado, o assassínio da velha senhora desperta nele as velhas tradições a que nunca ligou. Por outro, o seu colega é morto, o que obriga Ross a dividir-se pelos dois casos.

(c) Nascido a 4 de julho de 1946, Ron Kovic oferece-se aos 20 anos como voluntário para o Vietname, desejoso de servir o seu país. Ferido em combate, torna-se paraplégico e herói nacional. Escreve as suas memórias e é esta autobiografia que Oliver Stone (*Platoon*, *Wall Street*, *JFK*) – também combatente no Vietname – adapta, num filme que recebe o Oscar de melhor realizador. Para o papel do protagonista, Stone escolheu, contra a opinião de muitos, Tom Cruise, e o jovem ator é na composição da figura de Kovic.

13

É TUDO?

Is that everything?

In this unit you will learn

- how to obtain postal services
- how to buy groceries
- how to deal with car hire, parking and petrol

Diálogo 1

Sylvia has bought some postcards (**postais**), and goes to the post office (**correio**) to buy stamps.

Sylvia Bom dia. Quanto custa enviar um postal para Inglaterra por favor?

Empregada 2 reais e cinqüenta centavos.

Sylvia E este pacote? Por via aérea?

Empregada Ponha na balança. Agora, pesa um quilo e cem gramas, então custa 7 reais e noventa centavos.

Sylvia Bom, então queria seis selos para postais, e quero enviar o pacote também.

Empregada São 22 reais e noventa centavos no total.

Sylvia Aqui tem uma nota de cinqüenta.

Empregada (counts change) Agora dez centavos dá vinte e três, vinte e quatro, vinte e cinco, trinta, e vinte dá cinqüenta.

Sylvia Obrigada. Onde é a caixa?
Empregada É ali à direita, ponha no lado esquerdo, onde diz 'estrangeiro'.

enviar *to send*	**pesa** *it weighs*
postal(o)/postais *postcard/s*	**quilo(o)** *kilo*
pacote(o) *parcel*	**gramas(os)** *grammes*
por via aérea *by air mail*	**no total** *in all*
ponha *put*	**caixa(a)** *post box*
balança(a) *weighing scales*	**estrangeiro(o)** *abroad*

Diálogo 2

Next Sylvia goes to a local grocery store (a **mercearia** or **mini-mercado**) to buy some food for her few days away in the countryside.

Dono (owner) Bom dia. Pois não?
Sylvia Bom dia. Queria pão por favor. Tem pãezinhos?
Dono Aqui. Quantos quer?
Sylvia Meia dúzia. E um pacote de manteiga.
Dono Que mais?
Sylvia Tem presunto?
Dono Temos este, que é muito bom, ou aquele (pointing), que também é saboroso.
Sylvia Me dê 250 gramas deste aqui por favor.
Dono Mais alguma coisa?
Sylvia Sim, tem um bom queijo?
Dono Este queijo é excelente. Quer provar um pedaço deste?
Sylvia Mmm, que delícia. Me corte meio quilo por favor.
Dono É tudo?
Sylvia Só faltam umas garrafas de água, uma de guaraná, que adoro, e estas coisinhas que tenho aqui no carrinho.
Dono Muito bem. São 36 reais no total. Obrigado e boa viagem.

pãezinhos(os) *bread rolls*	**só faltam** *there're just*
quantos? *how many?*	**que mais?** *what else*
meia dúzia *half a dozen*	**saboroso** *tasty*
pacote(o) *packet*	**deste** *of this*
excelente *excellent*	**mais alguma coisa?** *anything else?*
pedaço(o) *a bit*	**provar** *to taste*
é tudo? *is that everything?*	**que delícia** *delicious*

me corte *cut me*	**coisinhas(as)** *few things/little things*
garrafas(as) *bottles*	**carrinho(o)** *trolley*

Verdadeiro ou falso?

Answer **verdadeiro** or **falso** to these statements.

	V	F
(*a*) Sylvia quer comprar oito pãezinhos.		
(*b*) O senhor não tem presunto.		
(*c*) Sylvia prova um queijo antes de comprar.		
(*d*) Sylvia compra uma garrafa de cerveja.		

Gramática

1 *The quantities of shopping*

Weights and measures (metric of course!)

1k	**um quilo**	1l	**um litro**
½k	**meio quilo**	½l	**meio litro**
250g	**250 gramas**	250dl	**um quarto de litro**
100g	**100 gramas**		

Other quantities

um pacote	*packet*	**uma caixa**	*box*
um rolo	*roll*	**um tubo**	*tube*
uma barra	*bar*	**um frasco**	*jar*
uma lata	*tin, can*		

2 *One of this, some of those*

These expressions are often lifesavers when you do not know, or cannot remember the names of items. You can simply point and say:

um/uma
uns/umas } **destes/destas daqueles/daquelas** *one of these / those*

6, 10, etc. **um pouco** **um quilo**	destes/destas daqueles/daquelas

3 *This here, that there*

You have already learnt that **este** (**esta**) means *this* (*thing, here*), and **aquele** (**aquela**), means *that* (*thing there*). There are also the words **esse, essa, esses, essas,** which refer to the thing nearest the person with whom you are talking.

A **esta flor aqui**	B **essa flor aí (que você tem)**	C **aquela flor ali**
this flower here	*that flower you have there*	*that flower over there*

4 Quanto? *how much?*

Quanto is used as an adjective in expressions such as **quantos quer?** (i.e. **quantos pãezinhos**). If you were buying bottles, you would be asked **quantas? (garrafas**).

Used as a question (**quanto é/quanto custa/m/, quanto vale**) it doesn't change form.

5 *Groceries*

The following check list may be useful

os ovos	*eggs*	**os biscoitos**	*biscuits*
as balas	*sweets*	**os cereais**	*cereals*
o mel	*honey*	**o azeite**	*olive oil*
a farinha	*flour*	**o açúcar**	*sugar*
o molho	*sauce*	**a massa**	*pasta*

Sumário

Here is a summary of shopping expressions

Quanto custa?	*How much does it cost?*
Tem?	*Do you have?*
Quanto/a/os/as quer?	*How much / many do you want?*
Que mais?	*What else?*
Me dê/corte (Dê-me ...)	*Give / cut me*
Mais alguma coisa?	*Anything else?*
É tudo?	*Is that all?*
Pois não?	*Can I help you?*
São... no total	*That's ... in all.*
Este, esse, aquele	*this, that, that*

Dicas culturais

• The post office usually opens from 9–6 during the week, although some close for lunch. Postage is expensive in general, as is faxing. The queues are enough to try the patience of a saint, but in larger branches you can now buy stamps at the philatelic desk. You can recognise the Post Office by the ECT sign – **Empresa de Correios e Telégrafos**.

• Shops also open at the above times, with the smaller ones closing for lunch (between 11.30 a.m. and 2 p.m.). On Saturdays shops tend to close at lunchtimes, apart from the larger shopping centres and supermarkets.

Atividades

1 Fill in your part of this dialogue in a post office.

You	(Say *good afternoon, how much does it cost to send this parcel to Germany please*).
Empregada	Ponha na balança. Agora, dois quilos, então são 13 reais.
You	(Say *right, I'd like to send the parcel, and I would also like 10 stamps*)
Empregada	Para a Alemanha também?

You (Say *no, 3 for Spain and 7 for England*)
Empregada São 35 reais e setenta centavos.
You (Say *thank you, where is the post box?*)
Empregada É ali, à esquerda.

2 Look at Miguel's shopping list below, and then listen to his conversation at the **minimercado**. Tick off everything he buys, put a cross by what is not available, and write down in English the extra item he buys.

1/2 dúzia de ovos
açúcar
2 pacotes biscoitos
frasco de mel
presunto – 250 gramas
1 1/2 litros cerveja
8 pãezinhos

Extra item = ______________________

3 Fill in the gaps using the appropriate form of **este**, **esse** or **aquele**.

(*a*) _______ postal aqui é para minha amiga.
(*b*) Qual manteiga? _______ que você tem aí.
(*c*) _______ senhores ali são italianos.
(*d*) _______ pãezinhos aqui são muito bons.
(*e*) _______ balas que você tem são deliciosas.

4 Grocery bingo. Here is your Bingo card, containing five items of grocery. Listen to the voice on the tape, who will call out various items, and cross off those on your card when you hear them. When you've heard all five, shout Bingo! If you have done so correctly, you should hear the voice congratulate you (**parabéns**).

Diálogo 3

Sylvia goes to a hire-car agency.

Sylvia Boa tarde. Eu posso alugar um carro aqui?
Empregado Claro. Tem todos os documentos necessários?
Sylvia Aqui, tome.
Empregado Bom, estão todos em ordem. Agora, é para quantos dias?
Sylvia Para quatro, começando de hoje. Tem algo econômico, mas ao mesmo tempo confortável – quero ver um pouco da região.
Empregado Temos um Ford, que custa 53 reais por dia, mais 6 por quilômetro. O preço inclui o seguro.

Sylvia	Ótimo!
Empregado	Agora, é só assinar aqui, e pronto. Não se esqueça de trazer o carro de volta com o depósito enchido.

alugar *to hire, rent*
necessários *necessary*
em ordem *in order*
começando *beginning*
econômico *reasonable*
ao mesmo tempo *at the same time*
inclui *includes*
seguro(o) *insurance*
não se esqueça *don't forget*
de volta *back*
o depósito *tank*
enchido *full(filled)*

Diálogo 4

Whilst she is looking at a map, Sylvia is approached by a policeman (**um policial**).

Policial	Boa tarde. Sabe que é proibido estacionar aqui?
Sylvia	Ah boa tarde senhor policial. Ainda bem que está aqui. Parece que estou perdida. O que faço para chegar em Goiânia?
Policial	Goiânia é? Bom, o melhor é virar aqui para a esquerda, tomar aquela estrada, e continuar até ao próximo cruzamento. Depois vai ver os sinais.

proibido *prohibited*
estacionar *to park*
ainda bem *thank goodness*
perdida *lost*
o melhor é *the best thing to do is*
estrada(a) *mainroad*
cruzamento(o) *crossroads*
sinais(os) *traffic signs*

Diálogo 5

Later Sylvia stops for petrol.

Sylvia	Boa tarde. Ponha 15 litros por favor.
Empregado	De normal, sem chumbo, gasóleo ou de álcool?
Sylvia	Creio que é sem chumbo. É carro alugado.
Empregado	Ah sim, olhe aqui diz sem chumbo. Então 15 litros. É tudo?

Sylvia	É possível verificar a água e o óleo para mim?
Empregado	Claro. Um momento só. Pronto. Está tudo OK.
Sylvia	Obrigada.

normal *2-star petrol*
gasóleo *diesel*
sem chumbo *unleaded*
álcool *alcohol* (used in Brazil)
alugado *hired*
olhe *look*
aqui diz *here it says*
verificar *to check*
óleo(o) *oil*
pronto *right then*

Gramática

1 Por

The preposition **por** *for* is used in expressions with prices, e.g. **reais por dia** *reais per day*. **Por** contracts into pelo, pela, pelos and pelas when combined with the article. Eg. **vou pela cidade** = *I'm going through (by) the town.*

2 Verbs – adjectives

O depósito enchido/estou perdida/carro alugado, are all examples of verbs used as adjectives. You can do this by using what is called the 'past participle'. This is the part in English such as 'seen, broken, parked, opened', etc. In Portuguese, it is formed in the following way:

FAL[AR] remove ending
FAL + **ado** (**ar** verbs) or **ido** (**er/ir** verbs)
FALADO = *spoken* **COMIDO** = *eaten*
PARTIDO = *departed, left, broken*

Be careful with irregular verbs. Here are some examples:

ver	visto	vir	vindo
fazer	feito	abrir	aberto
escrever	escrito	pagar	pago

Rules of adjectives then apply. For example:

a casa é feita de madeira	*The house is made of wood*
as janelas estão partidas	*The windows are broken*

You will come across past participles again, in use as part of a past tense in Portuguese.

3 O melhor é *The best thing to do is*

This construction can be used with a variety of adjectives as well as with **melhor** (*best*).

O importante é	*The important thing is*
O pior é	*The worst thing is*
O triste é	*The sad thing is*

Dicas culturais

• Petrol – sugar cane alcohol is the normal fuel, although diesel is also very common. Many roads are terrible, some not more than dirt tracks. You may well need a credit card to hire a car, unless you have reais in cash. Insurance in Brazil may not give you full cover, so do be aware of what you are signing for.

Atividades

5 Now see if you can do the following:

(*a*) Ask if you can rent a car here.
(*b*) Say it's for 8 days, starting today.
(*c*) Ask what you do to arrive in Rio.
(*d*) Say I seem to be lost.
(*e*) Say put in 12 litres of alcohol please.
(*f*) Ask can you check the water for me.

6 Choose an appropriate past participle for each sentence from the box and make any necessary alterations to it to use it as an adjective.

(*a*) O banco está _______
(*b*) Todas as janelas estão _______
(*c*) Os sapatos são _______ de couro
(*d*) A conta já está _______
(*e*) A carta está _______, senhor Mendes

aberto	pago	feito	fechado	escrito

7 Listen to someone at a petrol station and indicate on the grid the services they acquire.

Petrol – tick which type	How much?	Check water/oil	Price
Alcohol/Unleaded/Diesel			

8 **Estou perdido...** Fill in the gaps in this dialogue by inserting a word in place of each instruction.

Policial Good morning ________ ________. É prohibited ________ estacionar aqui nesta town square ________.

Sra. Desculpe. Acho que estou lost ________. O que faço para chegar no Rio ________?

Policial Bom, o melhor é virar aqui para a right ________, seguir até aos signs ________, e depois tomar a 2ª ________ à left ________, e continuar naquela motorway ________.

Compreende?

Can you link up the roadsigns with their corresponding instructions?

(a)		i) Área Escolar
(b)		ii) Aeroporto
(c)		iii) Vento Lateral
(d)		iv) Cuidado Animais
(e)		v) Semáforo à Frente
(f)		vi) Siga em Frente
(g)		vii) Vira à Direita
(h)		viii) Proibido Virar à Esquerda
(i)		ix) Proibido Trânsito de Bicicletas
(j)		x) Siga em Frente ou à Esquerda
(k)		xi) Velocidade Máxima Permitida
(l)		xii) Pedestra Ande pela Esquerda

14

ESTÁ LIVRE AMANHÃ DE TARDE?

Are you free tomorrow afternoon?

In this unit you will learn

- how to make plans for the future
- how to make arrangements to meet people
- how to deal with a telephone call
- months of the year

Diálogo 1

Sylvia overhears two people discussing their week-end plans whilst she is in a café in Campinas.

Moço (Boy) Que vai fazer sábado de manhã Teresa?

Moça (Girl) Gostaria de fazer aquela viagem para o Pantanal, já que temos férias neste momento. Quer vir comigo?

Moço Eu quero sim. Ouvi dizer que é uma viagem fantástica, a gente viaja no trem da morte, há-de ser super-legal.

Moça Não posso esperar – sempre quis ir. Sabe que a gente pode ver animais – há jacaré e tudo. Vamos até a Bolívia e depois voltamos. Leva mais ou menos uma semana para ir voltar.

Moço Ótimo. Olhe, eu aos sábados, costumo ir ao mercado bem cedo com minha mãe, mas estou livre a partir das oito e meia. Onde nos vamos encontrar?

Moça Na Rodoviária. Temos que ir primeiro a Sampa para apanhar o trem. Eu estarei lá às nove horas. Tá?

Moço Tá bem. A gente se vê no sábado. Tchau.
Moça Tchau. E não se esqueça da máquina fotográfica, tá?

gostaria de *I would like to*
o Pantanal *swamp area near Bolivia*
já que *seeing as*
férias(as) *holidays*
neste momento *at the moment*
ouvi dizer *I heard that*
a gente = nós *we*
viaja *travel*
há-de ser *it's bound to be*
super-legal *brill/mega*
esperar *to wait*
sempre quis ir *I've always wanted to go*
animais(os) *animals*
jacaré(o) *alligator*
leva *it takes*
costumo *I usually*
bem cedo *really early*
a partir das *from*
encontrar *to meet*
temos que ir *we have to go*
Sampa *São Paulo*
estarei *I will be*
tá = está? *OK*
a gente se vê *we'll see each other*
máquina fotográfica(a) *camera*

Diálogo 2

Back in her hotel, Sylvia has a call from a university aquaintance.

[ringing...]

Sylvia Alô
Nelson Alô, Sylvia?
Sylvia Sim, quem fala?
Nelson Daqui fala Nelson Gusmão, da Unicamp.
Sylvia Oi Nelson, tudo bem?
Nelson Eu estou muito bem. E você?
Sylvia Tudo azul. Como sabia meu número?
Nelson Foi o José que me disse. Então, como vai sua grande 'tour' do Brasil?
Sylvia Estou adorando. Estou fazendo boas amizades e desfrutando do tempo para explorar o país.
Nelson Bom, você esta livre amanhã de tarde?
Sylvia Estou sim. Tenho que fazer um trabalho até ao meio-dia, mas depois estou livre. Por quê?
Nelson Por que não vamos jogar tênis?
Sylvia Está bem. A que horas nos encontramos?
Nelson Às 2.30. Passo pelo hotel para te pegar. OK?
Sylvia OK. Até amanhã.
Nelson Tchau. Até amanhã.

alô *hello* (on phone)
daqui fala *this is*
Unicamp *University in Campinas*
tudo azul *everything just fine*
tempo(o) *the time*
explorar *to explore*
sabia *you knew*
disse *told*
amizades(as) *friendships*
desfrutando *taking advantage of*
passo *I'll pass*
pelo hotel *by the hotel*

Gramática

1 *Future plans* IR + *verbs*

The easiest and most common way of talking about future actions is to use the verb **IR** *to go* plus the infinitive of any verb. We do the same in English – *I'm going to visit Italy next summer.* / *We're going to buy a car next week.*

Remind yourself of the formation of **IR** from unit 3.

Vou visitar minha tia na semana que vem.	*I'm going to visit my aunt next week.*
Jaime vai comprar um livro amanhã.	*James is going to buy a book tomorrow.*
Vamos ganhar na loteria no sábado.	*We're going to win the lottery on Saturday.*

2 *Future plans – future tense*

You can also use the future tense, of course, to discuss your future actions, although in practice it is used less in spoken Portuguese. It can be used to emphasise particularly important actions. It is formed in the following way:

To the inifinitive of any verb add: **-ei** **-emos**
-á **-ão**

e.g. **comprarei** *I shall buy*
falarão *they / you* (pl) *will talk*

However, there are three exceptions:

fazer = **FAR** + endings
trazer = **TRAR** + endings
dizer = **DIR** + endings

All other verbs follow the regular pattern – a welcome relief to all learners! In dialogue 1, the girl said **estarei lá** – *I shall be there*. She could also have said **vou estar lá**, and even just **estou lá**. In colloquial Portuguese, it is common to substitute the present tense for the future.

e.g.	**Compro um carro amanhã**	*I'll buy a car tomorrow*
	Te vejo no domingo	*See you on Sunday*

3 *Future plans – future times*

You will need some time phrases to express your future actions.

amanhã	*tomorrow*
depois de amanhã	*the day after tomorrow*
a semana/o mês/o ano que vem	*next week / month / year*
o/a próximo/a semana, mês, ano	*next week / month / year*
domingo/no sábado, etc.	*Sunday / on Saturday, etc.*

4 Gostaria – *conditionals*

Gostaria is an example of a verb in what is termed a 'conditional' form. In English, we use the word *would* in conditionals. If you think that conditional actually means there is a 'condition' imposed on the action, it may help you to understand these structures. For example, *I would buy a car* (but I don't have the money). IF I had the money is the condition. With the example of the verb *to like*, the condition may be seen in terms of *I would like to*...IF that's OK/IF I may. Conditionals do lead into a complex part of Portuguese verb usage, however the actual formation is as straightforward as that of the future tense.

Infinitive +	**-ia**	**-íamos**
	-ia	**-iam**

(**Fazer** becomes **faria**, **trazer** becomes **traria**, and **dizer** becomes **diria**.)

Eu compraria um carro	*I would buy a car*
Maria falaria com ele	*Mary would speak with him*

As an alternative to **gostaria** in colloquial Portuguese, you may also hear **gostava/gostava/gostávamos/gostavam**. You will meet these forms again in unit 17.

5 Há-de ser/tenho que *obligation – must*

In Portuguese there are various ways to express obligation or *having to do something*. The most commonly-used in the spoken language is **TER QUE** or **TER DE**, as in Sylvia's **tenho que fazer um trabalho**... In English we would say *I've got to*... Stronger obligation is expressed through the verb **DEVER** *to have to/must*. Here it is almost your duty to do something.

Devo terminar este trabalho antes de sair.	*I must finish this work before going out.*

And in expressions such as:

Eles devem estar perdidos.	*They must be lost.*

There is also the use of the verb **HAVER** *to have*, plus **DE**, which conveys even stronger duty, something which is really bound to happen.

hei-de	hemos de
há-de	hão-de

For example:

Hei-de ganhar na loteria	*I've just got to win the lottery.*
Há-de ser bom	*It's bound to be good.*

6 A partir de

When you want to say 'from [a certain point] onwards' you use **a partir de** plus a point in time. This can be with the time: **a partir das duas horas** – *from 2 o'clock*, or time phrases: **a partir de domingo** – *from Sunday*/**a partir do mês que vem** – *from next month*, etc.

7 The gerund – -ING

In unit 6 you met this formation: **ando/endo/indo**. Sylvia uses a few examples to talk about what she is currently involved in doing: **Estou adorando..., fazendo..., desfrutando...**

With the verb **ESTAR**, this structure conveys an action currently taking place. For example:

Eles estão falando.	*They are talking (now).*
Agora estamos dormindo.	*Now we are sleeping.*
Eu estou aprendendo português	*I am (currently) learning Portuguese.*

Dicas culturais

- The **pantanal** is a great swampland area bordering the central-west part of Brazil and into Bolivia. The train crosses the middle of it and offers hardy travellers a marvellous panorama of its wildlife – alligators, birds, insects and big cats abound.
- The **trem da morte**, or *train of death*, is the subject of many a traveller's tale – you need to watch your belongings, and be wary of people offering you food or drinks.
- Telephone calling – in Rio, particularly, the telephone booths are called **orelhão** *big ear*, because of their design (there is one on the cover of this book). In some you need to buy *discs* (**fichas**) in a local bar or kiosk, although phone cards are being introduced in many areas. The number 6 in phone numbers is referred to as **meia** (*half*) – half a dozen.

Atividades

1 Now see if you can do the following:

(*a*) Ask Paul what he's going to do on Wednesday afternoon.
(*b*) Say you'll be there at 10.30.
(*c*) Suggest to your friend that you go swimming.
(*d*) Ask someone what time you'll be meeting.
(*e*) Say you're free from 4.15 onwards.
(*f*) Answer the phone and ask who's calling.

2 Listen to this telephone conversation between two friends and answer the questions that follow it.

(*a*) Who is calling?
(*b*) From where?
(*c*) When does he want to see his friend?
(*d*) What will Paulo be doing?
(*e*) What does Paulo's friend suggest?
(*f*) What time will he pick Paulo up?
(*g*) Where?

3 Make sentences by choosing words from each box, and forming the correct part of the future tense. A variety of answers may be correct. You will find samples in the Key.

	TIME	PERSON	ACTION	END
(*a*)	amanhã	Cristina	visitar	um bolo
(*b*)	o mês que vem	eles	comprar	na loteria
(*c*)	no domingo	eu	escrever	Alemanha
(*d*)	o próximo ano	a sra Lopes	ganhar	uma carta
(*e*)	depois de amanhã	nós	fazer	um carro

4 Decide what is currently going on in each picture, and write it under each one, forming the correct parts of **Estar** and the gerund.

(a)(Eles)[ESTAR]______. (b)(A Sra)[ESTAR]______. (c)(Nós)[ESTAR]______.

(d)(Eu)[ESTAR]______. (e)(Elas)[ESTAR]______.

Diálogo 3

After their tennis game, Sylvia and Nelson chat over drinks.

Nelson Que outras cidades vai visitar?

Sylvia Bom, só me faltam seis semanas aqui, e quero visitar o sul.

Nelson Tem que visitar Rio Grande do Sul – a região dos gaúchos e as grandes fazendas. No sul também há bastante indústria.

Sylvia Sim, gostaria muito de ver Curitiba e também as cataratas de Iguaçu.

Nelson Vai adorar. Nesta época não tem tantos turistas – os meses piores são durante nosso verão – dezembro, janeiro e fevereiro.

Sylvia Ótimo. Então sem dúvida visitarei Iguaçu – são as mesmas cataratas que aparecem no filme 'A Missão' – acerca dos jesuítas portugueses e suas atividades com os índios aqui.

Nelson Bom filme. Então Sylvia, um brinde para o resto da sua viagem. Tchin tchin, e boa viagem.

Sylvia Saúde, e obrigada.

gaúchos(os) *cowboys/ranchers*
fazendas(as) *ranches/farms*
indústria(a) *industry*
cataratas(as) *waterfalls*
época(a) *season*
tantos *so many*
turistas(os) *tourists*
os meses piores *the worst months*
durante *during*
verão(o) *summer*
dezembro *December*
janeiro *January*
fevereiro *February*
sem dúvida *without doubt*
as mesmas *the same*
A Missão *The Mission*
jesuítas(os) *Jesuits*
índios(os) *Indians*
brinde(o) *a toast*
o resto *the rest*
tchin tchin *cheers*
saúde *cheers*

Gramática

1 Outro, tanto, mesmo

All of these words change their endings depending on the nouns to which they are referring.

outro	outra	outros	outras	*other/s*
tanto	tanta	tantos	tantas	*so much/many*
mesmo	mesma	mesmos	mesmas	*same*

Tanto in this form only can also be used with verbs, to give more information about the action, e.g. **ela fala tanto** – *she talks so much*. This usage is known as the adverb. **Mesmo** can also mean *self*: **Ela mesma vai comprar a casa** – *she herself is going to buy the house*.

2 Os meses *The months*

janeiro	*January*	**julho**	*July*
fevereiro	*February*	**agosto**	*August*
março	*March*	**setembro**	*September*
abril	*April*	**outubro**	*October*
maio	*May*	**novembro**	*November*
junho	*June*	**dezembro**	*December*

In Brazil they are written with a small letter.

3 As estações do ano *The seasons*

o verão	*summer*	**o outono**	*autumn*
o inverno	*winter*	**a primavera**	*spring*

Remember that Brazil's summer coincides with winter in the northern hemisphere.

4 Celebratory expressions

tchin tchin/sáude *cheers*
parabéns *congratulations*
boa viagem *bon voyage*
feliz aniversário *happy birthday*
boa sorte *good luck*
feliz natal *Happy Christmas*
feliz ano novo *Happy New Year*
as melhoras *get well*
boas férias *have a good holiday*
feliz páscoa *happy Easter*

Sumário

que vai fazer amanhã?	*what are you doing tomorrow?*
está livre amanhã/sábado?	*are you free tomorrow/Saturday?*

gostaria (gostava) de ver/visitar...	*I'd like to see / visit...*
leva uma hora/um mês	*it takes an hour / month*
estou livre a partir de...	*I'm free from...*
alô/quem fala?/daqui fala...	*hello / who's speaking? / it's ... here*
a que horas nos encontramos?	*at what time shall we meet?*
estou viajando/trabalhando	*I'm travelling / working*
saúde/boa viagem	*cheers / bon voyage*
verão/outono/inverno/primavera	*summer / autumn / winter / spring*

Atividades

5 Answer these T/F questions based on Dialogue 3.

	T	F
(*a*) Sylvia still has 7 weeks left in Brazil.		
(*b*) Rio Grande do Sul is a region of farms and industry.		
(*c*) At the moment there are not many tourists about.		
(*d*) The worst months are in the spring.		
(*e*) Sylvia wants to visit a Jesuit Mission.		
(*f*) Nelson toasts the rest of Sylvia's journey.		

6 Look at the following situations and what people are saying. They have become mixed up. Can you decide which expression belongs with which picture?

a)

b)

c)

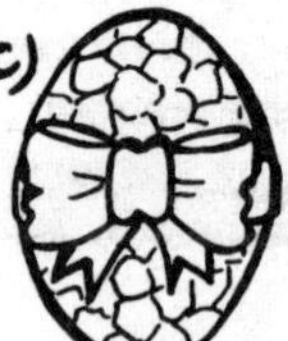

(i) feliz pásco　(ii) feliz aniversário　(iii) feliz natal
(iv) as melhoras　(v) parabéns　(vi) boa viagem

Compreende?

Your friend has sent you a cutting from a paper about a place she would like to visit with you. Look at the piece and insert the correct words from the box to fill the gaps. Then answer the questions below.

flores	festas	Estados Unidos
novembro	ano	cores

1) What kind of activity is this? music/sport/nature
2) What can you see there?
3) What is new this year?
4) When was the event originally set up?

FLORES

Roselândia apresenta festas na primavera

da Redação

Acontecem até o próximo dia 17 de ________ na Roselândia (km 33 da rodovia Raposo Tavares), as_____ da Primavera e das Rosas.

Realizados desde 1954, os eventos mostram novidades em rosas, _____ e plantas ornamentais provenientes da Europa e dos_______ _______ que a Roselândia introduz no Brasil.

Neste ____ além dos jardins com novas variedades de rosas, a novidade são as petúnias, com 15_____diferentes.

Informações pelo tel. (011) 7924-0122. (SC)

15

COMO FOI A VIAGEM?

How was the journey?

In this unit you will learn

- how to talk in the past
- how to discuss a visit you have made
- how to describe actions

Diálogo 1

Sylvia overhears some people talking about their holiday.

Sr Então, gostou da viagem? Visitou a catedral?

Sra Adorei. A catedral de lá é tão bonita e típica da arquitetura portuguesa. O nordeste é uma mistura interessante do africano com o europeu – a cultura, a música, e a religião.

Sr E as pessoas também – pele negra ao lado da branca, olhos pretos, azuis e verdes, cabelos escuros e claros – realmente é o que eles chamam uma miscelânia de culturas.

Sra Ficamos uma semana na Bahia, uns dias em Salvador e outros em Fortaleza. Assistimos a uma exibição de capoeira na praia, e falamos com os pescadores com suas jangadas.

Sr Comeram a comida de lá?

Sra Meu marido provou muitos pratos – vatapá por exemplo, mas eu achei um pouco picante.

Sr Então, valeu a pena?

Sra Sem dúvida! Esperamos voltar o ano que vem.

gostou? *did you enjoy?*	**o que eles chamam** *what they call*
visitou? *did you visit?*	**ficamos** *we stayed*
adorei *I loved*	**assistimos** *we watched*
tão *so*	**capoeira(a)** *acrobatic dance*
arquitetura(a) *architecture*	**falamos** *we spoke*
mistura(a) *mixture*	**pescadores(os)** *fishermen*
o africano *African*	**jangadas(as)** *Northeast boats*
o europeu *European*	**comeram?** *did you* (pl) *eat?*
cultura(a) *culture*	**comida(a)** *food*
religião(a) *religion*	**provou** *tasted*
pessoas(as) *people*	**pratos(os)** *dishes*
pele negra *dark skin*	**achei** *I found/thought*
olhos(os) *eyes*	**picante** *spicy*
cabelo(o) *hair*	**valeu a pena?** *was it worth it?*
sem dúvida *really, without doubt*	**Esperamos** *we hope*

Exercício

Choose the correct answers to these statements:

1) The lady visited a) the north. b) the south. c) the northeast.
2) In Bahia they stayed a) a week. b) a few days. c) two days.
3) She thought the food was a) too bitter. b) too spicy. c) too bland.

Gramática

1 *The past*

You have already met one or two expressions where the verb was in the past. To describe an action which was a one-off event, finished, complete, we use what is called the *simple past* (sometimes referred to as the preterite). In the dialogue, there were various examples, such as:

visitou *visited* **ficamos** *we stayed* **comeram** *you ate*

Let's look at how the regular **ar/er/ir** verbs are formed.

First you need to remove the **-ar** bit, and add the following endings on to the stem:

FAL(AR)	COM(ER)	PART(IR)
+ ei	i	i
ou	eu	iu
amos	emos	imos
aram	eram	iram

Can you spot ending patterns, like you did with the present tense? eg. **amos/emos/imos**. Note that the Brazilian forms in the *we* person are the same in the present and the past tenses. You may have to deduce what time zone an event took place in by looking carefully at the context, and searching for clues, such as 'yesterday', 'last night', etc.

Ela falou comigo.	*She spoke with me.*
Comemos muito.	*We ate a lot.*
Partiram às nove horas.	*They* (*you* pl.) *left at nine o'clock.*

In Portuguese this tense also translates as *have, has done*. So **falei com ela** can be *I spoke to her*, or *I've spoken to her*.

2 Past Questions

Did you notice the man's questions – **gostou?/visitou?/comeram?** – simply used the past part of the verb, with no equivalent of the English *did*. So the questions actually say *you liked...?/you visited...?/you ate...?*

3 O africano/o europeu

You have learnt that *o* + *adjective* is used to convey *the ... thing*, e.g. **o importante**. The example in our dialogue here is very similar:

o africano – *that which is African*
o europeu – *that which is European*

This structure is much neater than saying the whole phrase.

Diálogo 2

Back in her hotel, Sylvia chats to the receptionist.

Recepcionista Quando voltou de Porto Alegre?

Sylvia	Voltei ontem à noite. Apanhei o ônibus das 17 horas e cheguei aqui às 9:30.
Recepcionista	Gostou da visita?
Sylvia	Fiquei encantada. Visitamos uma fazenda, andamos a cavalo e comemos com os gaúchos.
Recepcionista	Comeu churrasco?
Sylvia	Sim, e bebemos um chimarrão, que é o chá típico da região.
Recepcionista	No inverno daqui, até os estudantes bebem este chá nas aulas por causa do frio aqui.
Sylvia	Que interessante. Bom. Tem algum recado para mim?
Recepcionista	Deixe ver. Ah sim, o senhor Ferreira acaba de telefonar. Disse que não é urgente.
Sylvia	Está bem, obrigada.

ontem à noite *last night*
fiquei *I became/was*
aulas(as) *lessons*
por causa de *because of*
recado(o) *message*
acaba de *has just*
urgente *urgent*

Diálogo 3

Sylvia returns José's telephone call.

Sylvia	Alô, José?
José	Alô, Sylvia tudo bem? Acabo de ligar para aí.
Sylvia	Eu sei. Me deram o recado agora.
José	Então, como foi a viagem pelo norte?
Sylvia	Foi ótima. Vi tantas coisas interessantes.
José	Foi a Manaus?
Sylvia	Fui, vi o teatro, dei uma voltinha pelo rio – fiz muitas coisas.
José	Foi à fazenda aí?
Sylvia	Sim, acabo de voltar. Os gaúchos são fascinantes – a maneira de viver, a cultura e o Fandango.
José	Dançou também?
Sylvia	Não me atrevi – eles dançam tão rapidamente, eu fiquei sentada.
José	Quando volta para cá?

Sylvia Bom, amanhã vou para Curitiba, depois visitarei uma amiga num cafezal. Daqui a duas semanas estarei de volta em São Paulo.
José Ligue para mim antes de partir. Tchau.
Sylvia Tchau.

acabo de ligar *I've just rung*
deram *they gave*
vi *I saw*
fui *I went*
dei uma voltinha *I made a little trip*
maneira(a) *way*
viver *to live/living*
Fandango *Fandango dance*
dançou? *did you dance?*
não me atrevi *I didn't dare*
dançam tão rapidamente *they dance so quickly*
sentada *sat down/seated*
cafezal(o) *coffee plantation*
ligue para mim *ring me*

Gramática

1 Past tense – awkward spellings

Some verbs alter their spellings in the past tense, to maintain certain sounds (hard or soft letters). In the dialogues you had: **cheguei** – from **chegar**. Other examples of this type are: **jogar** – **joguei**, **pagar** – **paguei**. This applies to the first person only.

Fiquei – from **ficar**. Other examples of this type are: **explicar** – **expliquei**, **tocar** – **toquei** (*I played/touched*), **indicar** – **indiquei**.

Other verbs also make changes in their spelling. Try to learn them as you come across them, and check in a grammar book for the patterns to learn.

Irregular simple past tense verbs

DAR	DIZER	FAZER	ESTAR	IR	PODER	PÔR
dei	disse	fiz	estive	fui	pude	pus
deu	disse	fêz	esteve	foi	pôde	pôs
demos	dissemos	fizemos	estivemos	fomos	pudemos	pusemos
deram	disseram	fizeram	estiveram	foram	puderam	puseram

SABER	SAIR	SER	TER	TRAZER	VER	VIR
soube	saí	fui	tive	trouxe	vi	vim
soube	saiu	foi	teve	trouxe	viu	veio
soubemos	saímos	fomos	tivemos	trouxemos	vimos	viemos
souberam	saíram	foram	tiveram	trouxeram	viram	vieram

2 Acabar de – *to have just done*

This handy expression is easy to learn, and very useful. You use the present tense of the verb **acabar** (*to finish*), plus **DE** plus a verb in the infinitive. For example:

Sr Ferreira acaba de telefonar *Mr Ferreira has just telephoned*
Eu acabo de chegar *I've just arrived*

3 Aí – *there (where you are)*

It is slightly confusing knowing when to use the various words for *here* and *there*.

Aqui	**Aí**	**Ali**
Cá		**Lá**
Here	*There*	*There*
(where I/we are)	(where you are)	(where neither of us are)

These also correspond to the demonstratives you learnt in unit 13:

Este	**Esse**	**Aquele**
this here	*that near you*	*that over there*

So if you are talking to someone on the phone, you must use **aí** if you want to say e.g. *is it warm there?* – **está quente aí?** If you say **está quente lá?**, you are referring to somewhere distant from your listener.

4 *Slow, slow, quick quick slow*

Adverbs, as you learnt previously, give us more information about a verb. They answer the question *how?* For example: *They dance. How do they dance? Quickly.*

In English many adverbs end in *-ly*.

Eles dançam. COMO dançam? Rapidamente.

In Portuguese many adverbs end in **-mente**.

To form an adverb, take the feminine form of an adjective and add **-mente**. If there is no separate feminine form, add **-mente** to the standard form. For example:

rápido – rápida – rapidamente
fácil – facilmente

There are some irregular adverbs, including:

mal *badly* **bem** *well* **devagar** *slowly* **cedo** *early*

Sumário

gostou de...?	*did you like...?*
visitou a catedral/a praia?	*did you visit the cathedral / beach?*
como foi a viagem?	*how was the trip?*
foi ótimo/maravilhoso/péssimo	*it was great / brilliant / awful*
voltei/apanhei/comi	*I returned / caught / ate*
tem algum recado para mim?	*do you have any messages for me?*
...acaba de telefonar/ligar	*...has just phoned*
daqui a duas semanas	*in two weeks time*
falam rapidamente	*they speak quickly*
ligue para mim	*give me a ring / call*

Atividades

1 Can you do the following?

(*a*) Ask your friend if she visited the museum.
(*b*) Say we stayed two weeks in Italy.
(*c*) Ask José and Sônia when they returned from New York.
(*d*) Ask the receptionist if he has a message for you.
(*e*) Say I've just arrived in the hotel.
(*f*) Say the Italians speak so quickly.

2 Complete the sentences with the correct form of the past tense of the verb in brackets.

(*a*) Ontem eu (comer) muito.
(*b*) No ano passado eles (comprar) uma casa.
(*c*) Nós (partir) à meia-noite.
(*d*) Vocês (gostar) da festa?
(*e*) Marcelo (escrever) um postal para sua mãe.

3 Choose the correct verb in each sentence.

(*a*) Ela viu/veio João no mercado.
(*b*) Eu fui/fiz um belo jantar.
(*c*) Nós pudemos/pusemos os pratos na mesa.
(*d*) Eles foram/fizeram ao cinema.
(*e*) Você trouxe/teve boa sorte.

4 Complete your part of the dialogue about a visit.

Ricardo Quando voltou do Rio?
You (say *I returned yesterday afternoon. I arrived here at 3.25*)
Ricardo Gostou da visita?
You (say *yes, a lot. I walked on Copacabana beach, visited Sugar Loaf Mountain – Pão de Açúcar, and I saw the shanty towns –* **as favelas**.)
Ricardo Gostou da comida também?
You (*say yes, I ate* **feijoada** *and tried the firewater and lime drink.*)

5 Form the correct past tense and choose an adverb from the box, to go with the pictures overleaf.

rapidamente	devagar	bem	cedo	mal

6 Listen to the dialogue, and fill in the gaps with the words you hear.

José Então, como foi a viagem para _______?
Sylvia Foi ótima. Vi tantas coisas interessantes.
José Foi a Londres?
Sylvia Fui. Fui ao _______, vi o Big Ben, _______ o _______ – fiz muitas coisas.
José Foi à _______ também?
Sylvia Sim, acabo de voltar. Os _______ são _______ – a maneira de viver, a cultura e a _______.
José Dançou também?
Sylvia Não me atrevi – eles dançam tão rapidamente, eu fiquei sentada.
José Quando volta para cá?
Sylvia Bom, amanhã vou para _______, depois visitarei uma

	amiga. Daqui a _______ estarei de volta em _______.
José	Ligue para mim antes de partir. Tchau.
Sylvia	Tchau.

Compreende?

Read Teresa's letter and see if you can answer the questions on it.

Minas, 10 de julho de 19..

Oi Cecilia, tudo bem?

Acabo de voltar das férias que passei nos Estados Unidos. Foi super-legal. Fiquei com meus tios, que moram na California. O tempo estava super-quente e gostei imensamente.

Fomos visitar muitos lugares interessantes, e vi as casas enormes dos atores de Hollywood. Passei em frente da casa de Michael Jackson - parece um castelo! Um dia viajamos até Disneyworld, onde passamos muitas horas divertindo-nos. Nunca vi tantas pessoas na vida! Provei a comida de lá - é tudo comida-rápida, tipo hamburguer e batatas, não é nada saudável. Comprei uma recordação para ti, acho que vai adorar.

Ouvi muita música americana, e na última noite fui a uma discoteca, que legal! A única coisa que realmente detestei foi a falta de guaraná!

Eu te digo mais no sábado, ligue para mim antes de vir,

tchau,

Teresa

1) Onde foi de férias?
2) Como estava o tempo?
3) Viu a casa de quem?
4) Que pensa da comida?
5) Onde foi na última noite?
6) Que detestou mais?
7) Quando vai ver Cecilia?

16

QUANTO CUSTARAM?

How much did they cost?

In this unit you will learn

- how to talk about what you have bought
- how to identify your own property
- further practice with the past

Diálogo 1

Sylvia listens to some people discussing what they have just bought.

M1 Que quadros mais lindos! Onde os comprou?

F Comprei-os numa lojinha no fim daquela rua ali. A senhora foi super-simpática comigo. Ela me deu um desconto porque comprei dois. Gosta Paulo?

M2 Gosto. São paisagens típicas do sul. Quanto custaram?

F Não muito. Só 35 reais cada. Uma pechincha, não acham?

M1 Realmente!

F E você, Carlos, comprou alguma coisa?

M1 Nós fomos até à feira-hippy. Nunca vi tantas coisas bonitas. Que difícil escolher!

F E daí – que decidiu?

M1 Vi estas pedras preciosas, que adorei, e depois compramos esta caixinha de madeira.

F Que bonitinha! Quanto custou? Foi cara?

M2 Não, só 13 reais.

F Puxa! Eu preciso ir lá já. Onde é que fica esta feira?

que quadros mais lindos! *what beautiful pictures!*
lojinha(a) *small shop*
no fim *at the end*
simpática *kind/nice*
paisagens(as) *landscapes*
quanto custaram? *how much did they cost?*
cada *each (one)*
pechincha(a) *a bargain*
a feira hippy *hippy/craft fair*
nunca vi *I've never seen*
escolher *to choose*
e daí? *and so?*
que decidiu? *what did you decide?*
caixinha(a) *small box*
foi cara? *was it expensive?*
puxa! *crikey!*

Exercício

Can you answer the following in Portuguese?

(*a*) Que comprou a senhora? _______
(*b*) Onde foram os dois senhores? _______
(*c*) O que Carlos adorou? _______

Gramática

1 *Exclamations*

It's nice to be able to inject exclamations into your dialogues, where relevant, as this makes your Portuguese much more authentic. Portuguese is a very expressive language, and the Brazilians especially love using it in a vibrant and sometimes vociferous way!

These few expressions will suffice for now to get you started:

Que + noun + adjective: **Que vestido lindo!** *What a nice dress!* Or, using **mais**: **Que vestido mais lindo!** *What a gorgeous dress!*

Que coisa mais linda!	*What a lovely / gorgeous thing – isn't it gorgeous!* (very common)
Que legal!	*Brill / mega / wicked!*
Ótimo!	*Great / brill / mega / wicked*
Puxa!	*Gosh!*
Nossa!/nossa senhora	*Our Lady / crikey*
'Vij'/Virgem Maria	*Virgin Mary / flippin' heck* (quite strong)
E daí?	*And so / and then / and? / so what?*

2 Cada – *Each, every*

Cada is a handy word meaning *each* or *every*. It never changes form, thus you could have:

cada semana = todas as semanas	*every week*
cada dia = todos os dias	*every day*
cada um custou	*each one cost*

Diálogo 2

A lady approaches the table.

Sra Desculpem, mas acho que a senhora pegou meus óculos de sol. Deixei-os no balcão daquela loja de artesanato ali em cima há meia hora.
F O quê? Acho que a senhora está enganada. Estes óculos são meus.
Sra Mas são óculos especiais porque não vejo muito bem. Olhe, aqui tem a marca Medioc.
F Onde? Ah, sim agora que eu vejo – tem razão. Peço desculpa. Foi sem querer. Então, onde estão os meus?
M1 Aqui, na sua cesta. Que bagunçeira!
F Tem toda razão – Desculpe senhora, tá?
Sra Não importa. Bom dia.

desculpem *excuse me (to a few)*	**especiais** *special*
pegou *you took*	**marca(a)** *make*
balcão(o) *counter*	**foi sem querer** *I didn't mean to*
há meia hora *half an hour ago*	**cesta(a)** *basket*
enganada *mistaken*	**que bagunceira!** *what a mess-pot!*
são meus *they're mine*	

Gramática

1 Há + *time*

You can use **Há** + a time phrase to mean *ago*, e.g.

há meia hora	*half an hour ago*
há duas semanas	*two weeks ago*
há muito tempo	*a long time ago*

2 *Identifying your belongings*

In previous units you have practised the possessive pronouns *my, your, his, our,* etc. Remind yourself of them if you cannot remember. To identify or claim your property, or that of someone else, you use the same set of pronouns plus the verb **SER**:

estes óculos SÃO meus	*these glasses are mine*
esta casa É nossa	*this house is ours*

You can answer the question **DE quem é...?** *Whose is...?*, simply by saying:

é	meu/sua/nossos, etc.
são	de Maria
	dele/dela, etc.

Dicas culturais

• Many towns in Brazil have a weekly crafts fair, often referred to as the **feira hippy**. Here you can find a variety of hand-made products, leather goods, jewellery, the beautiful semi- and precious stones for which Brazil is renowned, pictures – watercolour (**aquarela**) and oil (**óleo**), wax items (**de cera**). Also, there are usually stalls selling food – often you will find **baianas** – the typical women from Bahia (o nordeste), dressed in flouncy white clothes, selling the kind of spicy food you would eat in Bahia. The **feira hippy** is a great place to buy presents, and a wonderful place to spend some time drifting around.

Sumário

que ... mais lindos!	*what beautiful...!*
onde comprou?	*where did you buy (them / it)?*
quanto custou/custaram?	*how much did it / they cost?*
que difícil escolher!	*how difficult it is to choose*

puxa!/que legal! *crikey! / ace!*
acho que está enganado/a *I think you're mistaken*
tem razão *you're right*
foi sem querer *it wasn't on purpose*
há uma hora/algum tempo *an hour / some time ago*
é meu/minha, são meus/minhas *it's / they're mine*

Atividades

1 Replace **cada** with an appropriate form of **todo**, and change the verb forms where this becomes necessary.

(*a*) Ela vai ao mercado [cada semana] _______
(*b*) Nós gostamos de viajar [cada ano] _______
(*c*) [cada um dos] _______ livros (custa) _______ R$10.
(*d*) Maria trabalha muito [cada dia] _______
(*e*) [cada pessoa] _______ (ganha) _______ um presente.
(*f*) Gosto de [cada mês] _______ do ano.

2 Fill in your part of this dialogue about an item you have bought.

Marco Que vestido mais lindo. Onde o comprou?
You (say I bought it at the hippy-fair in the square.)
Marco Quanto custou?
You (say not a lot. Only 42 reais. Do you like it?)
Marco Gosto. Foi uma pechincha.
You (Ask him if he bought anything.)
Marco Comprei este livro numa pequena livraria.
You (say what a most interesting book)

3 Complete the sentences with possessives according to the pictures and instructions.

(*a*)

[US] este _______ é _______

(*b*)

[ME] _______ _______ são _______

(*c*)

[JOSÉ] _______ _______ é _______ _______

(*d*)

[VOCÊ] _______ _______ é _______

(*e*)

[THEM, masc.] _______ _______ são _______

4 Listen to four people talking about when they did various activities, and fill in the table below.

Speaker	Did what?	How long ago?
1		
2		
3		
4		

Compreende?

Read the following dialogue and/or listen to it on the tape, then answer the questions on it.

Sra Desculpe, mas acho que o senhor pegou meu guarda-chuva. Deixei-o no restaurante Mineiro na praça há vinte minutos.
Sr O quê? Acho que a senhora está enganada. Este guarda-chuva é meu.
Sra Mas é um guarda-chuva especial. Olhe, aqui tem o nome da minha companhia – Empresa Tecnical Limitada.
Sr Onde? Ah, sim agora que eu vejo – tem razão. Peço desculpa. Foi sem querer. Então, onde está o meu?
Sra Ali, ao lado da porta daquela loja.
Sr Você tem toda razão – Desculpe tá?
Sra Não importa. Bom dia.

1 What has he picked up by mistake?
2 Where was it left?
3 When?
4 How is it recognised?
5 Where is the other one?

17

ERA TUDO DIFERENTE

It was all so different

In this unit you will learn

- how to talk about something you saw earlier
- how to identify a stranger
- how to recall how a place used to be

Diálogo 1

Sylvia pops back to a shop to buy a skirt she had seen in the window, but finds the display has changed.

Empregada Bom dia, pois não?

Sylvia Havia uma saia na vitrine de que gostei muito, mas já não está mais lá.

Empregada Como era a saia?

Sylvia Era azul com flores pequenas.

Empregada E onde estava exatamente?

Sylvia Estava à esquerda da vitrine, bem na frente.

Empregada E era de algodão ou de lã?

Sylvia De algodão. Era muito bonita. Acho que custava 56 reais.

Empregada Ah sim, agora estou me lembrando. Só tinha aquela e mais duas daquele modelo, e vendemos as três hoje de manhã.

Sylvia Ai que pena!

Empregada Quer ver as outras saias que temos?

Sylvia Não obrigada. Só queria aquela.
Empregada Está bem. Talvez haja mais na semana que vem.
Sylvia Está bem.

havia *there was*
mostra(a) *display*
vitrine(a) *shop window*
já não está *it's no longer there*
era *it was*
flores(as) *flowers*
estava *it was*
bem na frente *right in front*
custava *it cost*
estou me lembrando *I'm remembering*
tinha *there was*
modelo(o) *style*
vendemos *we sold*
que pena! *what a pity*
queria *I wanted*
talvez haja *perhaps there will be*

Gramática

1 Há/havia

Havia is the past equivalent of **há**. Remember you can use **há** to mean *there is/are*. Therefore, **havia** can mean *there was/were*. You may also come across the word **houve**, also meaning *there was/were*, but used to describe one-off happenings, such as:

houve um accidente	*there was an accident*
houve um barulho enorme	*there was a huge noise*
havia muitas pessoas na rua	*there were many people in the street*

Brazilians also use parts of **TER** for the same purpose, e.g. **teve um accidente/tinha muitas pessoas**.

2 *The past, part 2*

In unit 15 you learnt how to use the simple past to describe actions in the past which had been completed. In the dialogue here you are introduced to another past tense, called the *Imperfect*. It is called *imperfect* because usually there is no perfect ending to it – it's more open-ended than the previous past tense. It describes an action which was continuous in the past, going on for some time. Look at the examples from the dialogue:

Como era? (from **SER**)	*What was it like?* (all the time)
Onde estava (**ESTAR**)	*Where was it?* (all the time it was in the window)
Custava	*It cost* (all the time it had a price)
Só queria esta	*I only wanted this one* (all the time)

Compare these with verbs in the simple past:

Como foi o filme?	*What was the film like?* (as a whole/a report-back)
Ele me custou	*It cost me* (one-off payment)

It may help to look at the following 'time-line'.

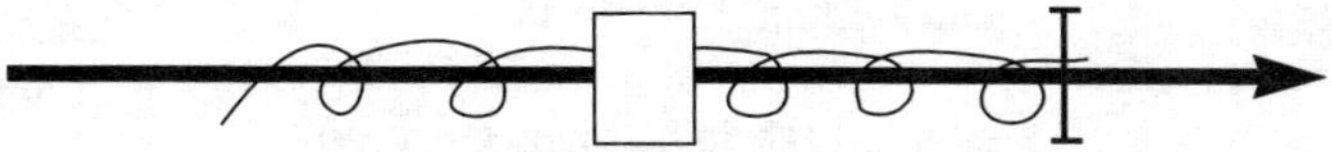

imperfect simple past NOW

The imperfect is a continuous line in the past, with often no clear ending (this can continue right up to the present time – I wanted it and I still do). The simple past is safely enclosed in a solid, complete box – it's finished. Often the simple past will interrupt an imperfect one, such as:

I was having a bath WHEN the phone rang.

(continuous) (sudden point) (simple)

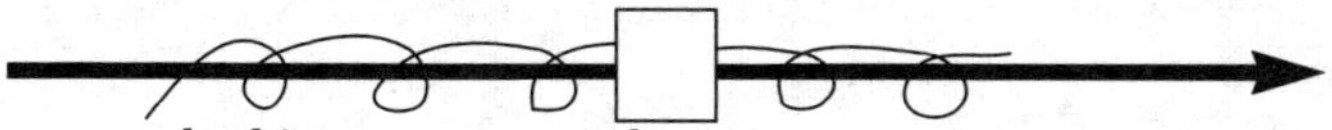

bathing phone

Formation

The imperfect tense is formed by taking the stem of the verb (the infinitive – **ar/er/ir**) and adding these endings:

FAL(AR)	COM(ER)	PART(IR)
ava	ia	ia
ava	ia	ia
ávamos	íamos	íamos
avam	iam	iam

e.g. **Ela falava comigo** *She was speaking to me*

Watch out for these irregular verbs:

Pôr	*to put*	punha, punha, púnhamos, punham
Ser	*to be*	era, era, éramos, eram
Ter	*to have*	tinha, tinha, tínhamos, tinham
Vir	*to come*	vinha, vinha, vínhamos, vinham

Diálogo 2

Sylvia has had a visitor at her hotel.

Recepcionista	Senhora Peters, havia um senhor aqui que a procurava.
Sylvia	Um senhor? Como era?
Recepcionista	Era bastante alto, tinha cabelo preto, um bigode, e estava vestido de terno cinzento.
Sylvia	Como ele se chamava?
Recepcionista	Não sei. Não disse o nome.
Sylvia	Mas o que ele queria?
Recepcionista	Também não sei. Só disse que voltava mais tarde.
Sylvia	Ele tinha que idade?
Recepcionista	Bom, provavelmente 50 e tantos anos.
Sylvia	Ah, já sei quem era. É o pai duma amiga minha que tem um cafezal aqui. Vou ficar uns dias com a família dela. Bom, vou subir.

procurava *was looking for*
como era? *what was he like?*
bastante *quite*
alto *tall*
bigode(o) *moustache*
vestido *dressed*
terno(o) *suit*
como ele se chamava? *What was he called?*
voltava *he would return*
idade(a) *age*
provavelmente *probably*
50 e tantos anos *50-odd*
pai(o) *father*
uma amiga minha *a friend of mine*
subir *to go up (stairs)*

Gramática

1 People descriptions

Notice which verbs were used in the descriptions.

ERA - SER – for permanent characteristics
TINHA - TER – possession, hair/eyes/beards, etc., age
ESTAVA - ESTAR – temporary characteristics/states, what they are wearing

If you want to describe people in detail, you will need:

height	**alto**/*tall* **médio**/*medium* **baixo**/*small, short*
build	**grande**/*large* **gordo** / *fat* **forte**/*strong* **pequeno**/*small* **magro**/*thin*
eyes	**os olhos** + colour
hair	**o cabelo** + colour **comprido**/*long* **curto**/*short* **liso**/*straight*
extras	**bigode**/*moustache* **barba**/*beard* **óculos**/*glasses* **careca**/*bald*
clothes	revise unit 7

2 Uma amiga minha – *more possessives*

To express *a ... of mine / of yours*, etc. place the noun first, followed by the appropriate possessive. For example:

uns sapatos seus	*some shoes of yours / his, etc.*
uma amiga nossa	*a friend of ours*

Diálogo 3

Sr Mendes shows Sylvia round the coffee plantation, and explains how things used to be.

Sr Tudo é muito diferente agora. Antigamente havia menos tecnologia, não havia tantas máquinas, e mais pessoas trabalhavam por aqui.

Sylvia Mas, não é mais fácil hoje em dia?

Sr Isso, sim, mas também é um pouco mais impessoal. Antes a gente falava muito, comíamos juntos, íamos a bailes nas outras fazendas, e ajudávamos uns aos outros. Hoje existe muito mais competição.

Sylvia E a cidade, mudou também?

Sr Mudou, sim. Todos os dias íamos ao centro, tomar um cafezinho, falar com amigos, e depois jogávamos cartas e a vida passava na valsa. Hoje é tudo movimento, rápido, dinheiro.

Sylvia Mas pelo menos tem uma bela fazenda.

Sr Sim, casa, família, boa comida e um estilo de vida que não tínhamos antes – sim tudo tem recompensa. Vamos ver os processos lá dentro?

Sylvia Vamos, e depois um bom cafezinho!

antigamente *before*
tecnologia(a) *technology*
máquinas(as) *machines*
trabalhavam *they used to work*
impessoal *impersonal*
íamos *we used to go*
bailes(os) *dances*
ajudávamos *we used to help*
uns aos outros *one another*
existe *there exists*
competição *competition*
mudou *it has changed*
jogávamos *we used to play*
a vida passava na valsa *life went with the flow*
movimento(o) *rush*
dinheiro(o) *money*
pelo menos *at least*
bela *lovely*
um estilo de vida *lifestyle*
tínhamos *we had*
recompensa(a) *reward*
processos(os) *processes*

Gramática

1 *The imperfect – the way we used to be*

Another function of the imperfect tense is to describe how things 'used to be' or things you 'used to do'. You can introduce statements with expressions like:

antes/antigamente/ no passado	*before / in the past*
quando era/éramos jovem/ jovens	*when I / we was / were young*

quando morávamos em	*when we used to live in*

Look at these examples:

Quando João morava na Índia, bebia chá todos os dias	*When John lived (used to live) in India, he drank (used to drink) tea every day.*
Antes de me casar, eu trabalhava num banco	*Before I married, I worked (used to work) in a bank.*

Sumário

havia...	*there was / were...*
já não está	*it's no longer (there)*
como era?	*what was it like?*
onde estava?	*where was it?*
só queria este/esta	*I only wanted this one*
o que (ele) queria?	*what did (he) want?*
era alto/gordo/forte	*he was tall / fat / strong (large)*
50 e tantos anos	*50-odd / 50-ish*
antigamente dançávamos	*we used to dance in the past*
um amigo meu/seu/nosso	*a friend of mine / yours / ours*

Atividades

1 Now can you do the following?

(*a*) say there was a blouse I liked in the shop window
(*b*) say it was on the right of the display
(*c*) say she was short, with long hair and blue eyes
(*d*) say he was probably 40 or so years old
(*e*) ask if it's not more interesting nowadays
(*f*) say we used to swim every day

2 Decide in each case whether the verb should be in the imperfect or the preterite (simple past) tense.

(*a*) Ontem eu fui/ia à cidade para comprar um selo.
(*b*) Quando era/fui jovem, Carlos fumava.
(*c*) Nós jantamos/jantávamos quando o telefone tocou.
(*d*) Antigamente eles comiam/comeram muito mal.
(*e*) Na semana passada ela veio/vinha à minha casa.
(*f*) Onde estava/esteve você quando eu te telefonei?

3 Listen to descriptions of people, and decide which articles of clothing go on each body.

4 Form the correct part of the imperfect tense for the verbs, and link them to the second part of the sentence.

Quando éramos jovens...

(*a*) IR ________ *i*) mais energia
(*b*) BRINCAR ________ *ii*) aos bailes
(*c*) TER ________ *iii*) férias com nossos pais
(*d*) ESTUDAR ________ *iv*) no campo
(*e*) PASSAR ________ *v*) todos os dias

5 Complete your part in this dialogue in a shop.

You (say *there was a shirt in the shop window, but it's not there now*)
Emp. Como era?
You (say *it was black and was made of wool*)
Emp. E onde estava exatamente?
You (say *it was on the left of the display, behind the trousers*)
Emp. Ah sim, lamento mas vendemos aquela ontem. Quer ver os outros modelos que temos?
You (say *no thanks. I only wanted this one*)
Emp. Está bem. Adeus.

6 Link up the following descriptions with the correct pictures.

(*a*) João é alto e forte. Tem cabelo curto e liso e um bigode. Está vestido de terno e chapéu.
(*b*) Sabrina é de estatura média e magra. Tem cabelo comprido. Usa óculos.
(*c*) Lúcia é baixa e um pouco gorda. O cabelo dela é liso e curto, e ela está vestida de saia e blusa.
(*d*) Maurício é alto e magro. É careca.

Compreende?

Read this excerpt from an interview with an Indian, and decide which verbs from the two boxes should fill each gap. You must choose between verbs in the imperfect and preterite (simple past) tenses and then answer the questions which follow.

era	defendia	brigava	estavam

cheguei	criei	achei
consegui	veio	começamos

O ÍNDIO JURUNA COM A PALAVRA

(Trechos de uma entrevista publicada no 'Folhetim', suplemento do jornal 'Folha de São Paulo', de 25-12-1977, gravada pelos jornalistas Sérgio Gomes, João Marcos Pereira e Cristina Vilares)

"Estou com três anos como chefe. Antes eu **1** chefe de batalhador, o chefe guerreiro, **2** todo o povo índio, porque naquele tempo a gente **3** muito. Quando eu **4** aí eu tirei todas as brigas. Depois eu **5** outro problema: da reserva. Eu estava sabendo que 800 índios **6** vivendo com 14 mil hectares. Então eu **7** muito pouco. Eu conheço também os limites, conheço mapa, mais ou menos, então eu achei muito pequena essa reserva. Aí eu aumentei para 180 mil hectares. Vou lutando e defendendo o direito do povo do Xavante. Eu falava com o governador do Mato Grosso, eu falava com o presidente do Incra, com o presidente da Funai, eu brigava com o Ministério do Interior. Falava com o vice-presidente da República. **8** O presidente, parece Costa e Silva, criou o decreto da terra dos Xavantes. Depois **9** o dr. Emílio também decretou outra vez. O presidente Geisel fez sair todo o mundo: tirou fazendeiro, tirou posseiro, tirou tudo. Nós **10** marcar limite, assim com picada, para poder tirar o pessoal.'

	T	F
(*a*) He has been the chief for 3 years.		
(*b*) When he arrived, 800 indians were living on 14,000 hectares of land.		
(*c*) He thought the reserve was too big.		
(*d*) He spoke to the President of Brazil.		
(*e*) The land was designated Xavante land.		
(*f*) The text is taken from a TV interview.		

18

O QUE VOCÊ TEM?

What's the matter?

In this unit you will learn

- how to describe illness and ailments
- how to deal with the chemist and doctor
- how to cope with an accident
- how to say goodbye

Diálogo 1

Sylvia has returned to the Ferreira's house in São Paulo, but has woken up not feeling very well.

Sylvia Marlí, não me sinto nada bem.
Marlí O que você tem?
Sylvia Estou com dor de barriga e tenho uma dor de cabeça.
Marlí Parece muito pálida. Vou chamar nosso médico. Fique aí na cama até ele chegar.
[40 minutos mais tarde]
Médico Onde dói senhora Peters?
Sylvia A barriga e a cabeça. Os olhos também me doem.
Médico Que comeu ontem?
Sylvia Ontem à noite saímos a um restaurante e eu comi um arroz com mariscos.
Médico E em geral tem algum problema quando come peixe?
Sylvia Geralmente não. É grave?

Médico Não se preocupe senhora Peters. Creio que é só uma pequena alergia. Fique onde está, na cama até sábado, e tome este medicamento.

não me sinto nada bem *I don't feel at all well*
o que você tem? *what's the matter?*
me dói/doem *my...hurts/hurt*
barriga(a) *belly*
dor(a) *pain*
cabeça(a) *head*
pálida *pale*
médico(o) *doctor*
fique *stay*
cama(a) *bed*
até ele chegar *until he arrives*
saímos *we went out*
um arroz com mariscos *seafood risotto*
grave *serious*
não se preocupe *don't worry*
creio que *I think/believe that*
alergia(a) *allergy/reaction*
medicamento(o) *medication*

Verdadeiro ou falso?

True or false?

	T	F
(*a*) Sylvia has a sore stomach.		
(*b*) Her teeth also hurt.		
(*c*) Last night she ate steak and rice.		

Gramática

1 Feeling ill

To express ailments, you can use the verb **doer** *to hurt* in the following way:

Indirect Object Pronoun + DOER + part/s of body

me	**dói**	**a cabeça** = *my head hurts*
lhe	**doem**	**os olhos** = *his / her / your eyes hurt*

What you are doing is saying that X gives pain TO you/him, etc.

You can also use: **TER uma dor de** _______
TER uma dor em _______
ESTAR com dor de/no, na ___

These are most common in Brazil.

Tenho uma dor de cabeça	*I have a headache*
Ele tem uma dor nos olhos	*He has sore eyes*

Other ailments may include:

uma enxaqueca	*a migraine*
ter gripe	*to have a cold*
ter insolação	*to have sunstroke*
cortar	*to cut*
magoar	*to hurt*
bater	*to hit*

2 O corpo – *the body*

You cannot describe where your pain is adequately without knowing the parts of the body. Here is a body and head for you to study.

Diálogo 2

When she goes to the chemist (**a farmácia**) to pick up Sylvia's medicine, Marlí overhears another customer.

Farmaceûtico	Bom dia. Diga por favor.
Cliente	Tem alguma coisa para dor de garganta?
Farmaceûtico	Sim, temos estas pastilhas que são excelentes, ou este xarope.
Cliente	Levo as pastilhas.
Farmaceûtico	É só?
Cliente	Não, o que tem para queimaduras de sol?
Farmaceûtico	Hmm, este creme é bom. É só 2 reais e 40 centavos.
Cliente	Bom, levo dois frascos.
Farmaceûtico	Então, são 7,80 reais.
Cliente	Também preciso de alguma coisa para meus lábios – estão muito secos.
Farmaceûtico	Tem isto, que é novo – é um batom transparente que protege o lábio antes e depois do sol.
Cliente	Muito bem. Vou experimentar. Obrigada, é tudo.
Farmaceûtico	Agora são 8,45 reais. Adeus e espero que melhore!

tem alguma coisa para...? *do you have anything for...?*
garganta(a) *throat*
pastilhas(as) *pastilles*
xarope(o) *syrup*
o que tem para...? *what do you have for...?*
queimaduras de sol *sunburns*
creme(o) *cream*
lábios(os) *lips*
secos *dry*
novo *new*
batom(o) *lipstick*
proteje *protects*
antes e depois do sol *before and after sun*

Gramática

1 Medicines

Here are a few useful items you may need to purchase at the chemist's:

comprimidos	*pills*	**aspirina**	*aspirin*
uma ligadura	*bandage*	**um band-aid**	*plaster*
toalhas higiênicas	*sanitary towels*	**um colírio**	*eyewash*
repelente de insetos	*insectant repellant*	**antihistamínico**	*antihistamine*

2 Espero que melhore

This expression (*I hope that you get well*) introduces us to another area of verbs in Portuguese, which is extremely complex, and which causes the most concern to learners as they progress a little further. We are only going to touch lightly upon it as an introduction.

So far, you have learnt some different tenses of verbs, to help you talk in various time zones. Now we are going to look at something called the *Subjunctive*, which has also a set of tenses, but used in very different, and specific circumstances. One of these, in the present tense, is as you saw in the dialogue, after the verb *to hope*, or *to wish*, when you are wishing something for someone else.

Other uses include:

esperar QUE	*to hope/wish that*
duvidar QUE	*to doubt that*
sentir QUE	*to feel sorry that*
é possível QUE	*it is possible that*
é incrível QUE	*it is incredible that*
é provável QUE	*it is probable that*

The main feature is the word **QUE**, and it is the verb which FOLLOWS **que** that goes into the subjunctive form. You have in fact come across the subjunctive before, in the guise of Commands. Remember in unit 7, you learnt how the endings of -**AR** verbs became like -**ER** verbs, and those from -**ER** and -**IR** verbs, became like -**AR** ones? That is the formation of the present subjunctive. Here again to remind you are our three regular verbs:

FALAR	COMER	PARTIR
fale	coma	parta
fale	coma	parta
falemos	comamos	partamos
falem	comam	partam

As usual, watch out for irregulars! Look at these examples:

Espero que você coma bem	*I hope that you eat well*
Ela duvida que ele parta amanhã	*She doubts that he will depart tomorrow*
É impossível que elas escrevam tanto	*It's possible that they (should) write so much*

The Subjunctive is something that takes a long time to sink in, but at least with a small notion of it under your belt, you are armed to understand a little bit more of the structures that may be used in conversation with you.

Diálogo 3

On the way back home Marlí witnesses an accident. She goes over to the injured person.

Marlí Você precisa de ajuda?
Sr Obrigado. Tenho uma dor na perna. Acho que está partida. Que dor! Não posso mexer nada.
Marlí Que aconteceu?
Sr Eu estava atravessando a rua sem problemas; tinha chegado mais ou menos ao centro quando de repente – baf! um carro me bateu e aqui estou.
Marlí Parece que o carro não parou. Idiota! Bom, não se preocupe senhor. Vou chamar uma ambulância. Não demora muito.

Marlí uses the telephone in a nearby shop.

Marlí Alô, escute, houve um acidente na rua Moraes Sales.
Telefonista Tem alguém ferido?
Marlí Sim, um senhor, a perna foi quebrada quando um carro a bateu. Precisamos duma ambulância.
Telefonista Onde está exatamente?
Marlí Na rua Moraes Sales perto da praça Paulista, ao lado da igreja Santa Augusta. O nome do senhor é Paulo Mendonça.
Telefonista E seu nome senhora?
Marlí Eu sou Marlí Ferreira.
Telefonista Está bem. Uma ambulância está a caminho.

ajuda(a)	*help*	**quebrada**	*broken*
mexer	*to move*	**parou**	*stopped*
que aconteceu?	*what happened*	**idiota**	*idiot*
estava atravessando	*was crossing*	**demora**	*take a while*
tinha chegado	*had arrived*	**escute**	*listen*
de repente	*suddenly*	**ferido**	*injured*
bateu	*hit*	**foi quebrada**	*was broken*
		está a caminho	*is on the way*

Gramática

1 Imperfect

In unit 14 you saw how you could use the verb **estar** plus the gerund – the 'ing' part of the verb (**ando/endo/indo**) to make an action that is currently happening. You can also do this using the imperfect of **estar** and the gerund to describe an action in the past which was in the middle of happening, e.g. **Estava atravessando** *I was crossing*. This is used more commonly than the pure imperfect on its own – **atravessava** *I was crossing*.

2 The past part 3

If you want to describe an action which took place and was completed before another past action began, you use a tense known as the *pluperfect*. In English it corresponds to *had done*. Look at these examples in English:

When he arrived home, she had (already) gone out.
We were sure he had told us a lie.

And from the dialogue:

Tinha chegado... quando de repente — *I had arrived... when suddenly....*

This tense is often used in relating incidents, or giving a report of a sequence of events.

It is formed using the imperfect of **TER**, plus the past participle. For example:

Eles tinham comido muito	*They had eaten a lot*
Maria tinha falado com ele antes de sair	*Mary had spoken with him before going out*

3 The passive

With most actions, there are two ways of expressing what has happened. Look at these two examples:

1) **A perna (se) quebrou**	*The leg broke (itself)*
2) **A perna foi quebrada**	*The leg was broken (by...)*

Statement 1) is known as an *active sentence*, where the subject of the verb actively carries out the action. Statement 2) is called a *passive sentence*, because the subject in fact is acted upon by someone or something, known as the agent.

The passive is constructed using **SER** (in the simple past) plus the past participle of the relevant verb, used as an adjective. If you want to say who or what the agent was, you introduce it with **POR** (*by*). For example:

A janela foi fechada pela professora	*The window was closed by the teacher*
Os soldados foram mortos	*The soldiers were killed*
Eu fui mordido por uma abelha	*I was stung by a bee*

ESTAR and the past participle used as an adjective conveys the STATE something is in as a result of an action, e.g.

A janela estava fechada	*The window was closed*
Ele estava perdido	*He was lost*

Atividades

1 Can you now:

(*a*) Say that you don't feel at all well
(*b*) Ask your husband/wife where it hurts
(*c*) Ask if the chemist has anything for toothache
(*d*) Ask what he has for migraines

(*e*) Ask what has happened
(*f*) Tell the emergency services that there's been an accident on Campo street

2 Link up the statements with the pictures

(*a*) Tem alguma coisa para insolação?
(*b*) Dói-me a barriga
(*c*) João bateu o dedo
(*d*) Ela tem uma dor nos olhos
(*e*) Meu marido tem uma dor de cabeça
(*f*) Cortei a perna. Preciso dum band-aid

3 Link up the two parts of each sentence, and form the second verb (in brackets) in the subjunctive.

(*a*) Esperamos que	*i*) eles [ESTUDAR] tanto
(*b*) Sinto muito que	*ii*) nós [GANHAR] muito dinheiro
(*c*) É incrível que	*iii*) sua filha [MELHORAR]
(*d*) Ela duvida que	*iv*) Sonia [ESTAR] doente
(*e*) É possível que	*v*) ele me [AMAR]
(*f*) Espero que	*vi*) ele [VIR] hoje

4 Listen to the phone call to the emergency services and write down the following information.

Accident where? Name of caller?	How many injured?	Injuries?	Exact location?

5 Place the correct past form of the verb and give any other information required to complete the sentences.

(*a*) A escola ser/estar _______ [closed] _______ durante as férias.
(*b*) Os presentes ser/estar _______ [given] _______ aos turistas [by the hotel owner] _______.
(*c*) As portas ser/estar _______ [open] _______.
(*d*) Eu ser/estar _______ [invited] _______.
(*e*) A carta ser/estar _______ [written] _______ [by Luis] _______.
(*f*) Os sapatos ser/estar _______ muito [dirty] _______.

6 Complete your part of the dialogue at the chemist's.

You (ask *if the pharmacist has anything for a headache*)
Farm. Sim, temos estas aspirinas que são boas, ou tem estes comprimidos.
You (say *you'll take the aspirins*)
Farm. É só?
You (say *no, what do you have for allergies?*)
Farm. Tem este creme repelente, se é alergia a insetos, ou estes comprimidos antihistamínicos.
You (say *I'll take a bottle of the cream. How much is that please?*)
Farm. São 6 reais e 40 centavos por favor.
You (say *thank you and goodbye*)

Dicas culturais

• It's advisable to have any injections before you get to Brazil, drink only bottled water and avoid any shellfish which may not be freshly caught. Chemists can be extremely helpful; hospital treatment is chaotic, although there is an excellent hospital in São Paulo. Most medication is available, but take supplies if you are travelling inland or into the Amazon.

• Avoid undue contact with police if you can help it!

Diálogo 4

It's time for Sylvia to leave. The Ferreiras have taken her to the airport and are saying goodbye.

José Sylvia, foi tão bom te ver outra vez. Volte logo – sabe que tem uma casa aqui sempre. Será sempre bem-vinda.

Sylvia Obrigada José. E Marlí também, obrigada por tudo. Foi uma visita fantástica, e vocês foram muito generosos. Espero-os lá na Inglaterra, tá? A próxima vez vocês vão ficar conosco.

Marlí Foi um prazer te conhecer finalmente. José tinha falado tanto em ti. Volte sempre, e nossos cumprimentos ao resto da família. Leve consigo estes Cds da nossa música.

Sylvia Que legal! Gilberto Gil, Milton Nascimento, Simone, alguns dos meus músicos preferidos. Obrigada e até a próxima.

José Se Deus quiser.

Sylvia E se eu ganhar na loteria! Adeus. Tchau tchau!

volte logo *come back soon*
por tudo *for everything*
generosos *kind*
foi um prazer *it was a pleasure*
finalmente *finally*
em ti *about you*
músicos preferidos *favourite singers*
se Deus quiser *hopefully/god willing*
se eu ganhar na loteria *If I win the lottery*
volte sempre *come back again*

Sumário

não me sinto nada bem	*I don't feel at all well*
o que você tem?	*what's the matter?*
me dói/doem	*my ... hurt/s*
não se preocupe	*don't worry*
tem alguma coisa para...?	*do you have anything for...?*
o que tem para...?	*what do you have for...?*
espero que melhore	*I hope you get better*
que aconteceu?	*what (has) happened?*
houve um acidente	*there's been an accident*
volte sempre	*come back (again)*

REVISION EXERCISES ON UNITS 10–18

In this unit you will have further practice of the grammatical points and vocabulary items from units 10–18. You may wish to revise the Gramática sections before you begin, or use this unit as a progress test. All the answers are in the Key on page 201.

1 Form adverbs from the words in brackets.

(*a*) [súbito] _______ vi meu amigo na praça.
(*b*) [final] _______ os alunos terminaram o exame.
(*c*) Sai daqui [imediato] _______!
(*d*) Não entendo esta língua [fácil] _______.
(*e*) [aparente] _______, ela só tem treze anos!
(*f*) Ela está [temporário] _______ fora do país.
(*g*) Os dois irmãos cantam muito [mau] _______.

2 Change the verbs from the present tense to the preterite.

(*a*) Ela não [compreende] _______ muito.
(*b*) Todos os trenes [partem] _______ cada 30 minutos.
(*c*) Eu [vendo] _______ fotografias.
(*d*) Maria e Sonia [chegam] _______ de táxi.
(*e*) Pedro [está] _______ no hospital.
(*f*) Vocês [percebem] _______ tudo?
(*g*) Você [tem] _______ dinheiro?
(*h*) [tiramos] _______ as malas do hotel.

3 Form the imperfect tense correctly in these examples.

(*a*) Quantos anos [ter] _______ você quando foi para a Alemanha?
(*b*) Durante as férias nós [acordar] _______ tarde todos os dias.

(*c*) Eu [estar] _______ tomando banho quando ele telefonou.
(*d*) Eles [sentir-se] _______ cansados depois de trabalhar todo o dia.
(*e*) Ela só [querer] _______ comprar uma coisa – uma blusa amarela!
(*f*) Antigamente, ele [ir] _______ ao cinema cada semana.

4 Decide whether you should use **por** or **para** in each example, making any necessary changes to **por**.

(*a*) Vamos passar [por/para] _______ a praça.
(*b*) Quanto dinheiro ganha [por/para] _______ ano?
(*c*) A loja tem tudo [por/para] _______ crianças.
(*d*) A porta foi fechada [por/para] _______ a senhora.
(*e*) Eu vou [por/para] _______ a cidade.
(*f*) Eles fizeram um bolo [por/para] _______ mim.
(*g*) O banco fica [por/para] _______ aqui.

5 Choose the correct form of **ter**, and form the past participle of the verbs in capitals, to form sentences using the pluperfect tense.

(*a*) Maria e Lû	tinha	IR____ao cinema quando eu cheguei.
(*b*) Eu	tinha	COMPRAR——um novo carro.
(*c*) O professor	tinha	FALAR____muito antes de terminar a aula.
(*d*) Eu e José	tinham	COMER____pouco.
(*e*) Sra Guedes	tínhamos	SUBIR____ao quarto quando o marido telefonou.
(*f*) Vocês	tinham	VIVER____na França.

6 Change the verbs in capitals into the present subjunctive.

(*a*) Espero que você TER _______ uma boa viagem.
(*b*) Ana quer que o filho ESTUDAR _______ bem.
(*c*) Talvez ela FAZER _______ um bolo delicioso.
(*d*) Duvidamos que vocês ABRIR _______ seus livros hoje.
(*e*) É estranho que eles não IR _______ à escola.
(*f*) Talvez nós não FALAR _______ muito bem.
(*g*) Sinto muito que você ESTAR _______ doente.

7 Write the answers to these sums in full in Portuguese.

(*a*) 53 + 72 = _______
(*b*) 14 + 9 = _______
(*c*) 180 – 25 = _______
(*d*) 250 ÷ 5 = _______
(*e*) 46 + 362 = _______
(*f*) 841 + 659 = _______
(*g*) 1200 ÷ 20 = _______
(*h*) 5 × 500 = _______
(*i*) 25,364 – 63 = _______
(*j*) 123,801 + 99 = _______

8 Are the following numbers written correctly in Portuguese? If they are not, give the correct form in full.

	✓/✗	**correct version**
(*a*) 531 = quinhentos e trinta e um	☐	____________
(*b*) 1,250 = mil, duzentos e cinqüenta	☐	____________
(*c*) 348 = trezentos e quarenta e nove	☐	____________
(*d*) 96 = noventa e seis	☐	____________
(*e*) 5,221 = cinco mil, duzentos e trinta e um	☐	____________
(*f*) 26,860 = vinte e seis mil, novecentos e sessenta	☐	____________
(*g*) 72 = setenta e dois	☐	____________
(*h*) 28 = vinte e oito	☐	____________

9 Choose the appropriate past participle from the box for each sentence to form a passive. Make it agree with the noun.

(*a*) O gato foi _______ pelo cão.
(*b*) A porta foi _______.
(*c*) Eles foram _______ pelos soldados.
(*d*) O carro foi _______.
(*e*) As casas foram _______ pelo terremoto (earthquake).
(*f*) Eu (fem) fui _______.

morto
decepcionado
vendido
mordido
destruido
aberto

10 Can you find ten items of food or drink in this wordsearch?

O	B	M	E	Y	O	K	G	S	L
T	S	A	N	D	U	Í	C	H	E
N	O	L	E	I	T	E	Y	O	G
U	P	J	F	A	R	U	P	J	U
S	A	C	N	V	M	Ã	C	N	M
E	Y	O	E	Y	O	K	G	S	E
R	O	J	I	E	U	Q	R	U	S
P	A	Ç	U	C	A	R	U	P	J
F	A	C	N	W	T	I	L	H	D
Z	V	M	Q	R	O	H	N	I	V

11 Follow the numerical guidance, and fill in ten months of the year on the grid.

Across: 1 o décimo-primeiro mês
2 o quinto mês
3 o segundo
4 o quarto
5 o décimo-segundo
6 o sétimo

Down: 7 o primeiro mês
8 o nono mês
9 o terceiro
10 o décimo

12 Select an adjective from each box to form opposites.

(*a*) alto	(i) magro
(*b*) gordo	(ii) chato
(*a*) velho	(iii) feio
(*d*) interessante	(iv) horrível
(*d*) simpático	(v) baixo
(*f*) bonito	(vi) jovem

13 Can you find ten parts of the body on this wordsearch?

O	L	H	O	K	G	S	M	Ã	O
K	G	S	X	B	Q	R	U	P	J
F	A	C	N	Q	D	O	K	G	S
X	B	C	A	B	E	Ç	A	C	N
A	C	N	O	K	D	A	C	N	P
N	W	C	N	R	O	R	U	P	É
R	A	C	N	W	E	B	Q	R	U
E	Y	R	U	P	J	L	H	D	Z
P	J	F	I	L	H	D	H	D	Z
V	M	E	Y	Z	V	M	E	A	C

KEY TO EXERCISES

Unit 1

Verdadeiro ou falso?

(*a*) F (*b*) F (*c*) V

Exercício

(1) b (2) b (3) a

Exercício

(*a*) Boa, Bem, (*b*) é (*c*) muito

Atividades

1 (*a*) bom dia/boa tarde/boa noite (tarde (*b*) obrigado/a, tchau (*c*) sou/meu nome é X (*d*) Tem un apartamento reservado em meu nome? (e) Oi, tudo bem? **2** Aqui está. / Sim, sou. / Oito dias. / Tchau (adeus) **3** (*a*) sete (*b*) catorze (*c*) dezessete (*d*) onze (e) treze **4** (i) dezoito 18 (ii) dez 10 **5** (*a*) ii (*b*) iv (*c*) i (*d*) iii (e) v **6** (*a*) John Harris (*b*) Liverpool (*c*) 6 days (*d*) room 12

Compreende?

(1) female (2) false (3) true (4) en-suite (5) false

Unit 2

Verdadeiro ou falso?

(*a*) f (*b*) f (*c*) v (*d*) f (*e*) v

Verdadeiro ou falso?

(*a*) f (*b*) f (*c*) v

Atividades

1 Não, sou de Birmingham. / É grande e industrial. / Sim, tenho um filho. / Ele se chama David. Tem 28 anos e é professor de francês. / Sim, trabalho numa empresa internacional. **2** (*a*) iii (*b*) v (*c*) i (*d*) ii (e) iv **3** (1) a (2) b (3) b (4) a **4** (*a*) cinco/pequenas (*b*) brasileira (*c*) filhos interessantes (*d*) histórica (e) dois vinhos alemães

Compreende?

(1) 22-years-old (2) very big, modern, very interesting, (3) no (4) language student, school secretary
(5) Olá John,
Tudo bem? Eu estou muito bem. Vou te dizer um pouco sobre quem sou. Meu nome é Gary, tenho dezenove anos e sou de Bristol. É uma cidade

muito bonita – histórica, a turística. Sou casado e tenho um filho, Robert. Sou estudante de tecnologia.
Tchau, Gary.

Unit 3

Verdadeiro ou falso?

(*a*) f (*b*) t (*c*) t (*d*) t (*e*) f

Exercício

(*a*) sim (*b*) não (*c*) não

Atividades

1 (*a*) é (*b*) são (*c*) está (*d*) é (*e*) sou/sou **2** Não, sou de Brighton. / É uma cidade pequena ao sul de Inglaterra. / Sim é bastante perto. **3** (*a*) i (*b*) ii (*c*) ii (*d*) iii (*e*) iii **4** (1) Santos (2) Cantanduva (3) Campinas (4) Piracicaba (5) Uberaba

Compreende?

(1) f (2) f (3) v (4) f

Unit 4

Exercício

(*a*) no (*b*) yes (*c*) no

Verdadeiro ou falso?

(*a*) t (*b*) f (*c*) f

Exercício

(*a*) b (*b*) a (*c*) a

Atividades

1 (*a*) Há um açoügue por aqui? (*b*) Onde há um correio? (*c*) Que horas são? (*d*) São 2 e meia. (*e*) Na Alemanha chove pouco. **2** (*a*) iii (*b*) i (*c*) iv (*d*) ii (*e*) v **3** (*a*) farmácia (*b*) mercado (*c*) café Silvana (*d*) praça D.Pedro **4** (*a*) Mexico (*b*) Japan (*c*) Brazil (*d*) France (*e*) England **5** Desculpe, sabe se há um mercado aqui? / Sabe se está aberto agora? / São dez e um quarto (quinze). / Fica longe? / Obrigado/a, adeus (tchau). **6** (*a*) fica (*b*) ali (*c*) aqueles (*d*) terceira (*e*) para

Compreende

(1) post office (2) Gomes Sá Street (3) Nascimento Street (4) 4 p.m. (5) no

Unit 5

Exercício

(*a*) grande (*b*) num café (*c*) muito

Exercício

(*a*) f (*b*) v (*c*) f

Atividades

1 (*a*) saio de casa (*b*) começo o trabalho (*c*) 12.45 (*d*) 1.30 (*e*) 18.05 **2** (*a*) às sete e meia (*b*) às quinze para às nove (*c*) às duas e meia (*d*) às quatro e 25 (*e*) à uma e quinze (f) às dez para às oito **3** (*a*) A Alemanha **é a** cento e trinta e cinco quilômetros **da** França. (*b*) O Brasil **é a** mil, oitocentos e noventa e seis quil. **do** México. (*c*) A Inglaterra **é a** mil, duzentos e quarenta e sete quil. **de** Portugal. (*d*) Os Estados Unidos **são a** duzentos e oitenta e três quil. **do** Canadá. **4** (*a*) iii (*b*) i (*c*) v (*d*) ii (*e*) iv

Compreende?

(1) true (2) Portuguese (3) D (4) A (5) false (6) E – airport

Unit 6

Exercício

(*a*) sports/TV (*b*) sports/TV

(*c*) reading/music

Verdadeiro ou falso?

(*a*) t (*b*) f (*c*) t

Atividades

1 (*a*) ii (*b*) v (*c*) i (*d*) iv (*e*) iii **2** (*a*) conheço (*b*) sabe (*c*) sei (*d*) conhece (*e*) conhecem **3** Speaker 1=C, 2=A, 3=B **4** Adoro nadar, vou à piscina aos sábados. / Sim, um pouco. / Prefiro a música jazz. Francisco, o que você faz no tempo livre? / Também gosto do teatro, mas os ingressos são bastante caros.

Compreende?

1 Vinhos / Mary Black / High Street, no. 10 / CEP 23410 Centro / Southampton Hants. **2** (*a*) violão (*b*) mecânica geral (*c*) desenho artístico e publicitário

Unit 7

Exercício

C

Exercício

(*a*) sapatos (*b*) 39 (*c*) R85

Atividades

1 (*a*) ii (*b*) iii (*c*) i (*d*) vi (*e*) v (f) iv **2** Tem saias? / Acho que é o 42. / Tem em azul-claro? / Quanto é, (custa)? / Levo esta em azul e aquela em preto. / Obrigada **3** (*a*) compre / Buy the blouse! (*b*) comam / Eat the bread! (*c*) vão / Go through (*by*) here! (*d*) faça / Don't be noisy! (*e*) trabalhe / Work well! (f) falem / Don't talk a lot! **4** (*a*) boots (*b*) 39 (*c*) brown (*d*) too big (*e*) R98

Compreende?

(1) salads (2) eat fruits, not sweets, (3) make a dinner (4) have a good salt bath (5) relax a lot (6) massage

Unit 8

Exercício

(*a*) v (*b*) f (*c*) f

Exercício

(*a*) yes (*b*) no (*c*) yes

Atividades

1 (*a*) Tem uma mesa livre? (*b*) Somos cinco. (*c*) Não tenho sede. (*d*) Que vai pedir? (*e*) Garçom por favor. (f) A conta por favor. **2** (*a*) sigam (*b*) faça (*c*) beba (*d*) repitam (*e*) falem (f) traga **3** Para começar uma sopa de legumes. / Ovelha com arroz e salada. / Uma cerveja e uma jarra de água. **4** sobremesa / hoje / sorvete / baunilha / avelã / sim **5** (*a*) tenho fome (*b*) tem calor (*c*) temos sono (*d*) tem frio (*e*) têm sede **6** (*a*) iii (*b*) ii (*c*) i (*d*) iv **7** (*a*) dessert (*b*) drink (*c*) drink (*d*) starter (*e*) main meal (*f*) side dish (*g*) starter (*h*) side dish

Compreende?

Laura – creme de aspargos, omelete, fruta. Marcelo – canja, frango, doce de côco. Sérgio – lula frita, espeto misto, pudim caramelo. You – no starter, bife na brasa, sorvete. Rita – canja, peixe, fruta.

Unit 9

Atividades

1 (*a*) meus (*b*) sua/ a amiga dele (*c*) nossa (*d*) suas/ as irmãs delas (*e*) sua

2 (*a*) Pode me levar ao centro da cidade? (*b*) Boa viagem! (*c*) A que horas parte a próxima camioneta para o Rio? (*d*) Tem troco para uma nota de R50? (*e*) O que faço para chegar na praça Miraflores? (*f*) Conhece um bom restaurante aqui?
3 A que horas parte o próximo ônibus para Fortaleza? / Queria um bilhete de ida e volta. / Tem troco para uma nota de R100? / O ônibus sai de onde?
4 (*a*) iv (*b*) i (*c*) v (*d*) iii (*e*) ii
5 c/f/a/d/g/b/e/h

Compreende?

(1) T (2) F (3) F (4) T (5) T (6) F

Revision Unit 1

1 o/a/as/o/os uma/uns/umas/um/uma
2 (*a*) este (*b*) essa (*c*) Aqueles (*d*) destas (*e*) Esses (*f*) Aquela or Esta
3 (*a*) Tudo (*b*) Todas (*c*) todo (*d*) toda (*e*) tudo (*f*) Todas **4** (*a*) trinta e seis (*b*) cento e cinqüenta e dois (*c*) quinhentos (*d*) mil, trezentos e vinte e um (*e*) cinco mil e oitocentos (*f*) doze mil, seiscentos e cinqüenta e quatro (*g*) vinte e cinco mil, novecentos e noventa e nove (*h*) cem mil (*i*) catorze (*j*) novente e cinco
5 (*a*) 899 (*b*) 723 (*c*) 468 (*d*) 2,501 (*e*) 4,802 (*f*) 7,554 (*g*) 11,100 (*h*) 68,336 (*i*) 105 (*j*) 307 **6** (*a*) comem (*b*) falo (*c*) vai (*d*) parte (*e*) fazemos (*f*) viaja (*g*) escrevem (*h*) compreendem
7 (*a*) é (*b*) está (*c*) é/fica (*d*) estão (*e*) são/ficam (*f*) são (*g*) é/fica (*h*) é
8 (*a*) temo ii (*b*) há vii (*c*) temos viii (*d*) há iii (*e*) tenho vi (*f*) têm i (*g*) tem iv (*h*) há v **9** (*a*) Fale (*b*) coma (*c*) Feche (*d*) abram (*e*) Bebam (*f*) subam (*g*) começe (*h*) Preencha **10** (1) americanos (2) Inglaterra (3) espanhol (4) Brasil (5) França (6) alemães (7) gregos (8) Itália (9) chinês (10) Alemanha

11 (*a*) vestido (*b*) saia (*c*) calça (*d*) sapato (*e*) camisa (*f*) blusa (*g*) chapéu (*h*) luvas (*i*) casaco (*j*) gravata **12** vermelho/roxo/verde/azul/marrom/rosa/branco/preto/amarelo **13** Across: (1) supermercado (2) banco (6) sapataria (7) mercado (8) quiosque Down: (3) correio (4) açougüe (5) livraria (9) café (10) cinema.

Unit 10

Exercício

(*a*) R$360 (*b*) no (*c*) no

Exercício

Any 3 of: air-conditioning not working / tap won't close / pillow dirty / blinds don't open properly

Atividades

1 Boa tarde, tem um apartamento livre? / Simples por favor. Com banheiro. / Para três dias. / Quanto é por noite? / Está bem. Onde fica o apartamento? **2** (*a*) i or iii (*b*) i (*c*) v (*d*) iv (*e*) i, ii or iii (*f*) i (*g*) i **3** Twin/ with bathroom/3/Saturday/ 135/R$38 per person **4** (*a*) Desculpe, o garfo está sujo. (*b*) ... o ar-condicionado não está funcionando. (*c*) ... a torneira está pingando. (*d*) ... o prato está partido. (*e*) ... falta uma colher. **5** (*a*) ir (*b*) comer (*c*) terminar (*d*) ver (*e*) beber

Compreende?

(1) leaflet and gift (2) Villa Rossa, Hotel Santa Branca (3) Itambuca, Três Poderes (4) Full board (5) 3 (6) children up to 10-years-old in parents' room (7) Santa Branca (8) Três Poderes

Unit 11

Atividades

1 (*a*) odeia a rede (*b*) não gosto dos cachimbos (*c*) preferimos a cerâmica (*d*) gosta dos brincos (*e*) adoram os artigos de couro **2** (*a*) mim (*b*) deles (*c*) nela (*d*) si (*e*) você **3** (*a*) 1 (*b*) 2 (*c*) 1 (*d*) 2 (*e*) 2 **4** Estou procurando presentes para minha família. / Tem uma rede? / Quanto é? / Que tem para senhoras? / Vou levar a rede, e esta tapeçaria.

Compreende?

(1) 17 (2) from next year (3) 40 (4) school (5) guaraná and other soft drinks (6) o coelhinho, b quadrinhos, c aulas

Unit 12

Exercício

(*a*) Aliens (*b*) não (*c*) satírica (*d*) tarde (*e*) táxi

Atividades

1 (*a*) Por que não vamos ao museu? (*b*) A que horas começa o filme? (*c*) O concerto termina às dez horas (*d*) Que boa exposição! (*e*) Você é meu convidado João (*f*) Voltamos de ônibus? **2** (*a*) eu me (*b*) lhe (*c*) te (*d*) ele (*e*) lo **3** (*a*) ii (*b*) i (*c*) ii (*d*) Star Wars (*e*) 8.30 (*f*) i **4** Por que não vamos almoçar naquele barzinho ali? / Venha, eu te convido e sou e quem pago. / Insisto, você é meu/minha convidado/a. / Vamos.
5 (*a*) à cidade de ônibus (*b*) no avião da
(*c*) trem das 2 horas (*d*) de táxi a pé
(*e*) no carro de

Compreende?

Film A=iii / B=i / C=ii (*a*) A (*b*) B
(*c*) Vietnam (*d*) comedy (*e*) 2 (*f*) autobiography

Unit 13

Verdadeiro ou falso?

(*a*) f (*b*) f (*c*) v (*d*) f

Atividades

1 Boa tarde, quanto custa enviar este pacote a Alemanha por favor? / Bom, queria enviar o pacote e também queria dez selos. / Não, três para Espanha e sete para Inglaterra. / Obrigado/a, onde é a caixa? **2** Buys: ovos / biscoitos / presunto / cerveja / pãezinhos. / Not available: açúcar/mel. / Extra item: olive oil – azeite. **3** (*a*) este (*b*) essa (*c*) aqueles (*d*) estes (*e*) essas **4** As per tape **5** (*a*) Eu posso alugar um carro aqui? (*b*) É para oito dias, começando de hoje. (*c*) O que faço para chegar no Rio? (*d*) Parece que estou perdido/a. (*e*) Ponha doze litros de álcool por favor. (*f*) Pode verificar a água para mim? **6** (*a*) aberto or fechado (*b*) abertas or fechadas (*c*) feitos (*d*) paga (*e*) escrita
7 unleaded / 18 litres / no / R$11
8 Bom dia / proibido / praça / perdida / Rio / direita / sinais / segunda / esquerda / estrada

Compreende?

(*a*) ix (*b*) v (*c*) xii (*d*) i (*e*) x (*f*) iii (*g*) vi (*h*) ii (*i*) xi (*j*) vii (*k*) iv (*l*) vii

Unit 14

Atividades

1 (*a*) Que vai fazer quarta feira à tarde Paul? (*b*) Estarei lá às dez e meia. (*c*) Por que não vamos nadar?

(*d*) A que horas nos encontramos? (*e*) Estou livre a partir das quatro e quinze. (*f*) Alô, quem fala? **2** (*a*) Carlos Silves (*b*) Banco Brasil (*c*) Thurs a.m. (*d*) French lesson (*e*) golf (*f*) 11.45 (*g*) hospital **3** Examples: (*a*) Amanhã eu comprarei um carro. (*b*) O mês que vem nós visitaremos Alemanha. (*c*) No domingo Cristina fará um bolo. (*d*) O próximo ano eles ganharão a loteria. (*e*) Depois de amanhã a Sra Lopes escreverá uma carta. **4** (*a*) eles estão dormindo (*b*) ela está comendo (*c*) nós estamos estudando (*d*) eu estou andando (*e*) elas estão falando **5** (*a*) f (*b*) t (*c*) t (*d*) f (*e*) f (*f*) t **6** (*a*) vi (*b*) iii (*c*) i (*d*) ii (*e*) iv (*f*) v

Compreende?

(*a*) novembro (*b*) festas (*c*) flores (*d*) Estados Unidos (*e*) ano (*f*) cores (1) nature (2) roses, plants, flowers, (3) new variety of rose, 15 different colours of petunia (4) 1954

Unit 15

Exercício

(1) c (2) a (3) b

Atividades

1 (*a*) Visitou o museu? (*b*) Ficamos duas semanas na Itália. (*c*) Quando voltaram de Nova Iorque? (*d*) Tem algum recado para mim? (*e*) Acabo de chegar no hotel. (*f*) Os italianos falam tão rapidamente. **2** (*a*) comi (*b*) compraram (*c*) partimos (*d*) gostaram (*e*) escreveu **3** (*a*) viu (*b*) fiz (*c*) pusemos (*d*) foram (*e*) teve **4** Voltei ontem à tarde. Cheguei aqui às três e vinte e cinco. / Sim, muito. Andei na praia em Copacabana, visitei o Pão de Açúcar e vi as favelas. / Sim, comi feijoada e provei a caipirinha. **5** (*a*) Eles se levantaram cedo. (*b*) Ela correu rapidamente. (*c*) Elas cantaram mal. (*d*) Nós falamos devagar. (*e*) Eu toquei piano bem. **6** Inglaterra/ teatro/ visitei/ palácio/ Grécia/ gregos/ interessantes/ dança/ São Paulo/ 5 dias/ Brasília

Compreende?

(1) Estados Unidos. (2) Muito quente. (3) Michael Jackson e atores. (4) Não muito saudável. (5) Discoteca. (6) Falta de guaraná. (7) Sábado.

Unit 16

Exercício

(*a*) dois quadros (*b*) feira-hippy (*c*) pedras preciosas

Atividades

1 (*a*) todas as semanas (*b*) todos os anos (*c*) todos os ... custam (*d*) todos os dias (*e*) todas as pessoas ganham (*f*) todos os meses **2** Comprei-o (o comprei) na feira-hippy na praça. / Não muito. Só 42 reais. Gosta? / Comprou alguma coisa? / Que livro mais interessante! **3** (*a*) carro nosso (*b*) estas botas minhas (*e*) este gato de José (*d*) esta casa sua (*e*) estes livros deles **4** (1) went to Spain 2 years ago (2) visited Taj Mahal 3 months ago (3) had lunch ½ hour ago (4) went to cinema 5 days ago

Compreende?

(1) umbrella (2) restaurant Mineiro (3) 20 minutes ago (4) company name (5) shop doorway

Unit 17

Atividades

1 (*a*) Havia uma blusa na vitrine de que gostei. (*b*) Estava à direita da vitrine. (*c*) Ela era baixa, tinha cabelo comprido e olhos azuis. (*d*) Ele tinha provavelmente 40 e tantos anos. (*e*) Não é mais interessante hoje em dia? (*f*) Nadávamos todos os dias. **2** (*a*) fui (*b*) era (*c*) jantávamos (*d*) comiam (*e*) veio (*f*) estava **3** Body i = dress, long hair ii = t-shirt, skirt, short hair, glasses iii = hat, moustache, shirt, trousers **4** (*a*) íamos ii (*b*) brincávamos iv (*c*) tínhamos i (*d*) estudávamos v (*e*) passávamos iii **5** Havia uma camisa na vitrine, mas já não está. / Era preta e feita de lã. / Estava à esquerda da vitrine detrás das calças. / Não obrigado/a. Só queria aquela. **6** (*a*) iii (*b*) ii (*c*) i (*d*) iv

Compreende?

(1) era (2) defendia (3) brigava (4) cheguei (5) criei (6) estavam (7) achei (8) consegui (9) veio (10) começamos (*a*) t (*b*) t (*c*) f (*d*) f (*e*) t (*f*) f

Unit 18

Verdadeiro ou falso?

(*a*) t (*b*) f (*c*) f

Atividades

1 (*a*) Não me sinto nada bem. (*b*) Onde dói? (*c*) Tem alguma coisa para dor dos dentes? (*d*) (O) que tem para enxaquecas? (*e*) Que aconteceu? (*f*) Houve um acidente na rua Campo. **2** (*a*) iii (*b*) iv (*c*) v (*d*) vi (*e*) ii (*f*) i **3** (*a*) iii melhore (*b*) iv esteja (*c*) i estudem (*d*) vi venha (*e*) ii ganhemos (*f*) v ame **4** D Pedro square / 2 / broken arm, cut leg / corner with Main Street / Alexandra Esteves **5** (*a*) estava fechada (*b*) foram dados pelo dono (*c*) estavam abertas (*d*) fui convidado/a (*e*) foi escrita por Luís (*f*) estavam sujos **6** Tem, alguma coisa para dor de cabeça? / Levo as aspirinas. / Não, que tem para alergias? / Levo um frasco do creme. Quanto é por favor? Obrigado/a, adeus.

Revision Unit 2

1 (*a*) subitamente (*b*) Finalmente (*c*) Imediatamente (*d*) facilmente (*e*) Aparentemente (*f*) temporariamente (*g*) mal **2** (*a*) compreenderam (*b*) partiram (*c*) vendi (*d*) chegaram (*e*) esteve (*f*) perceberam (*g*) teve (*h*) Tiramos **3** (*a*) tinha (*b*) acordávamos (*c*) estava (*d*) sentiam (*e*) queria (*f*) ia **4** (*a*) pela (*b*) por (*c*) para (*d*) pela (*e*) para/pela (*f*) para (*g*) por **5** (*a*) tinham ido (*b*) tinha comprado (*c*) tinha falado (*d*) tínhamos comido (*e*) tinha subido (*f*) tinham vivido **6** (*a*) tenha (*b*) estude (*c*) faça (*d*) abram (*e*) vão (*f*) falemos (*g*) esteja **7** (*a*) Cento e vinte e cinco (*b*) Vinte e três (*c*) Cento e cinqüenta e cinco (*d*) Cinqüenta (*e*) Quatrocentos e oito (*f*) Mil e quinhentos (*g*) Sessenta (*h*) Dois mil e quinhentos (*i*) Vinte e cinco mil, trezentos e um (*j*) Cento e vinte e três mil e novecentos **8** (*a*) ✓ (*b*) ✓ (*c*) ✕ trezentos e quarenta e oito (*d*) ✓ (*e*) ✕ cinco mil, duzentos e vinte e um (*f*) ✕ vinte e seis mil, oitocentos e sessenta (*g*) ✓ (*h*) ✓ **9** (*a*) mordido (*b*) aberta (*c*) mortos (*d*) vendido (*e*) destuidas (*f*) decepcionada **10** sopa/pão/vinho/açúcar/legumes/ sanduíche/presunto queijo/ cerveja/leite **11** (1) novembro (2) maio (3) fevereiro (4) abril (5) dezembro (6) julho (7) janeiro (8) setembro (9) março (10 outubro **12** (*a*) v (*b*) i (*c*) vi (*d*) ii (*e*) iv (*f*) iii **13** braço/perna/cabeça/mão/olho dedo/boca/pé/orelha/nariz

BRAZILIAN PORTUGUESE –ENGLISH VOCABULARY

à direita *on the right*
à esquerda *on the left*
a pé *on foot*
abafado *close, hot*
aberto *open*
advogado/a *lawyer*
aeroporto (o) *airport*
agenda (a) *diary*
agora *now*
aguardente (o) *firewater*
álcool (o) *alcohol*
alô *hello*
amigos (os) *friends*
andar (o) *floor*
anos (os) *years*
antigo/a *old*
ao fundo *at the back*
ao lado de *next to*
aos sábados *on Saturdays*
apartamento (o) *room*
aquele/aquela *that*
aqui *here*
arroz de marisco (o) *seafood rice*
às vezes *sometimes*
aspirina (a) *aspirin*
até *until, up to*
avenida (a) *avenue*
avião (o) *aeroplane*
azeite (o) *olive oil*

banco(o) *bank*
banheiro (o) *bathroom*
barco (o) *boat*
barulhento/a *noisy*
bastante *quite*
batida (a) *milkshake*
bem *well*
bem-vindo/a *welcome*
bicicleta (a) *bicycle*
bilhete (o) *ticket*
blusa (a) *blouse*
bolsa (a) *bag*
bom *good, right then*
bonito *pretty*
botas (as) *boots*

cá *here*
cada ... *every ...*
café (o) *café / coffee*
café da manhã *breakfast*
caixa (a) *cash desk, till*
calças (as) *trousers*
cama (a) *bed*
camisa (a) *shirt*
canja (a) *chicken broth*
capoeira (a) *acrobatic dance*
cardápio (o) *menu*
carne (a) *meat*
caro *expensive*

carro (o) *car*
carteira (a) *wallet, purse*
casa (a) *house*
casado/a *married*
casal *couple, double*
cataratas (as) *waterfalls*
cavalo (o) *horse*
cedo *early*
centro (o) *centre*
chamo-me/me chamo *my name is*
chave (a) *key*
chega *arrives*
chope (o) *lager*
chuva (a) *rain*
cidade (a) *town, city*
clube (o) *social club*
coisa (a) *thing*
com *with*
come *he/she eats*
comemos *we eat*
comida (a) *food*
como é? *what is it like?*
comprar *to buy*
comprimido (o) *pill*
conhecer *to get to know*
contra *against*
cor (a) *colour*
correio (o) *post office*
couro (o) *leather*
cultura (a) *culture*
cultural *cultural*
custa *it costs*

daqui *from here*
de nada *don't mention it*
de onde é? *where are you from?*
de onde são? *where are you from?* (pl.)
de vez em quando *sometimes*
debaixo de *underneath*
deixar *to leave*
delicioso/a *delicious*
dentro *inside*
depois *then, after*
desculpe *excuse me*
dia (o) *day*
detrás de *behind*
difícil *difficult*
dinheiro (o) *money*
diz *says*
durante *during*
dúzia (a) *dozen*

e *and*
é *is*
em *in, on*
em frente de *in front of*
em geral *generally*
empresa (a) *business, company*
encher *to fill*
endereço (o) *address*
enorme *enormous*
então *well then*
entre *in between*
escola (a) *school*
escritório (o) *office*
Espanha (a) *Spain*
espanhois *Spanish* (pl.)
esquina (a) *corner*
está bem *O.K.*
estação (a) *station*
este/esta *this*
estilo (o) *style*
estou bem *I'm well*
estrada (a) *highway*
estudante *student*
eu *I*

fala? *do you speak?*
falo *I speak*
família (a) *family*
faça favor de... *please...*
farmácia (a) *chemist*
feijoada (a) *bean stew*
férias (as) *holidays*
fica *is situated*
ficar *to stay*
ficha (a) *form*
filha (a) *daughter*

filho (o) *son*
flores (as) *flowers*
fome (a) *hunger*
fora *outside*
França (a) *France*
frango (o) *chicken*
funcionar *to work*

garrafa (a) *bottle*
gasóleo (o) *diesel*
gasolina (a) *petrol*
gato (o) *cat*
gaúcho (o) *cowboy*
gente (a) *people*
gentil *kind*
geralmente *generally*
gosta/am? *do you like?*
gostam *they like*
gostamos *we like*
gostaria de *I would like to*
gosto *I like*
graças a Deus *thank goodness*
grande *big*
Grécia (a) *Greece*

há *there is, are*
há meia hora *½ hour ago*
havia *there was, were*
histórico *historical*
hoje *today*
hotel (o) *hotel*

ida e volta *return (ticket)*
ida (a) *single (ticket)*
idade (a) *age*
igualmente *likewise*
incluindo *including*
índios (os) *indians*
informações *information*
inglês/esa *English*
internacional *international*
interessante *interesting*
ir *to go*
irmã (a) *sister*
irmão (o) *brother*
isso *that's it*

jacaré (o) *alligator*
Japão (o) *Japan*
jogar *to play*
jornais (os) *newspapers*

lá, ali *there*
lamento *I'm sorry*
laranjas (as) *oranges*
leio *I read*
leite (o) *milk*
ler *to read*
levo *I'll take*
limão (o) *lime*
limpo *clean*
lindo *pretty*
linha (a) *platform*
litoral *coastal*
litro (o) *litre*
livros (os) *books*
loja (a) *shop*
Londres *London*
longe *a long way*

mãe (a) *mother*
maior *bigger*
mais de *more than*
mais ou menos *more or less*
mais tarde *later*
mala (a) *suitcase*
manteiga (a) *butter*
mapa (o) *map*
maravilhoso *wonderful*
marido (o) *husband*
mariscos (os) *seafood*
mas *but*
médico/a *doctor*
meio quilo *half a kilo*
melhorar *to improve*
mês (o) *month*
mesa (a) *table*
mesmo ali *right there*
moderno *modern*
momento (o) *moment*
mora *live*
moram *they, you live*

moro *I live*
mosquitos (os) *mosquitoes*
movimentado *busy*
muitas vezes *often*
muito *very*
muito bem *very well*
muito prazer *pleased to meet you*
mulher (a) *wife*
mundo (o) *world*
museu (o) *museum*
música (a) *music*

na *in / on the*
nadar *to swim*
não *no*
não funciona *it doesn't work*
neve (a) *snow*
nome (o) *name*
número (o) *number*
nunca *never*

o que faz? *what do you do?*
obrigado/a *thank you*
óculos (os) *glasses*
óleo (o) *oil*
ônibus *bus*
ontem *yesterday*
oportunidade (a) *opportunity*
ouço *I listen to*
outono (o) *Autumn*
outros (os) *the others*
ouvir *to listen to*
ovos (os) *eggs*

pacote (o) *packet*
pai (o) *father*
país (o) *country*
pais (os) *parents*
pão (o) *bread*
para *in order to / for*
para nós *for us*
parte *departs*
partido *broken*
passamos *we spend*
passaporte (o) *passport*
passar *to pass / spend*
pastelaría (a) *cake shop*
pedir *to ask for*
pegar *to get, catch*
pelo menos *at least*
pequeno/a *small*
peras (as) *pears*
perto *near*
pessoalmente *personally*
picante *spicy*
pingar *to drip*
pintar *to paint*
piscina (a) *swimming pool*
plástico *plastic*
podem *you* (pl.) *can*
podemos *we can*
pois *well*
poluição (a) *pollution*
pôr *to put*
por noite *per night*
por favor *please*
porque *because*
porta (a) *door*
porto (o) *port*
português/esa *Portuguese*
posso? *may I?*
postal (o) *postcard*
pouquinho (um) *a little bit*
praça (a) *square*
preciso de *I need*
preço (o) *price*
preencher *to fill in*
prefere *he she, you prefer(s)*
preferem *they, you prefer*
preferimos *we prefer*
prefiro *I prefer*
presunto (o) *smoked ham*
primeiro *first*
problema (o) *problem*
professor *teacher*
provar *to try, taste*
provavelmente *probably*
próximo *nearby*
puxa! *goodness*

quadro (o) *picture*
qual? *which?*
quanto é? *how much is it?*
quantos/as *how many?*
quarto (o) *¼ litre bottle*
quarto (o) *bedroom*
que *that, which*
que mais? *what else?*
que tal? *how about?*
queijo (o) *cheese*
quem? *who?*
quente *hot*
quer *wants*
quilo (o) *kilo*

rápido *fast*
recepção (a) *reception*
recomendo *I recommend*
refeições (as) *meals*
refeitório (o) *canteen*
refrigerante (o) *soft drink*
região (a) *region*
reservado *reserved*
reservar *to reserve*
revistas (as) *magazines*
roupas (as) *clothes*
rua (a) *road*

sabe? *do you know?*
saia (a) *skirt*
saida (a) *exit*
sanduíche (o) *sandwich*
sapatos (os) *shoes*
saudável *healthy*
saúde (a) *health*
se *if*
se Deus quiser *god willing*
selo (o) *stamp*
sem *without*
sempre *always*
senhores (os) *you*
sentar-se *to sit down*
sentir-se *to feel*
sim *yes*
sinais (os) *road signs*
sobremesa (a) *dessert*
sobrenome (o) *surname*
somos *we are*
sorvete (o) *icecream*
sou *I am*
sou de *I am from*
sujo *dirty*
suco (o) *fruit juice*

tamanho (o) *size*
também *also*
tão *so*
tarde (a) *afternoon*
táxi (o) *taxi*
tchau *bye*
telenovelas (as) *soap-operas*
televisão (a) *television*
têm *they have*
tem..? *do you have..?*
temos *we have*
tempo (o) *time*
tempo de lazer (o) *leisure time*
tempo livre (o) *free time*
tenho *I have*
terceiro *third*
terra (a) *land, hometown*
tipicamente *typically*
típico *typical*
todas as noites *every night*
todos os dias *every day*
tomar *to take*
trabalha *you work*
trabalho *I work*
transeunte *passer-by*
trocar *to change*
tudo *everything*
tudo bem? *O.K.?*

um pouco *a bit*
um pouco de *a bit of*
universidade(a) *university*

vago *free*
vários/as *various*
velho/a *old*
vende *sells*

vende-se/se vende *for sale*
vento (o) *wind*
ver *to see, watch*
verão (o) *summer*
vestido (o) *dress*
viagem (a) *journey*
vidro (o) *window, glass*
vinho (o) *wine*
vir *to come*
vista (a) *view*
vive *lives*

xarope (o) *syrup, remedy*

Números

um (uma)	1	vinte e um (uma)	21
dois (duas)	2	trinta	30
três	3	quarenta	40
quatro	4	cinqüenta	50
cinco	5	sessenta	60
seis	6	setenta	70
sete	7	oitenta	80
oito	8	noventa	90
nove	9	cem (cento)	100
dez	10	cento e um (uma)	101
onze	11	duzentos/as	200
doze	12	trezentos/as	300
treze	13	quatrocentos/as	400
catorze	14	quinhentos/as	500
quinze	15	seiscentos/as	600
dezesseis	16	setecentos/as	700
dezessete	17	oitocentos/as	800
dezoito	18	novecentos/as	900
dezenove	19	mil	1 000
vinte	20	un milhão	1 000 000

primeiro/a, 1º/1ª	*first*	sexto/a	*sixth*
segundo/a 2º/2ª	*second*	sétimo/a	*seventh*
terceiro, a, 3º/3ª	*third*	oitavo/a	*eigth*
quarto/a, 4º/4ª	*fourth*	nono/a	*ninth*
quinto/a 5º/5ª	*fifth*	décimo/a	*tenth*

— GRAMMAR INDEX —

Verbs

Grammar